COACH ROYAL

Voices and Memories™

Coach Royal

Conversations with a Texas Football Legend

DARRELL ROYAL WITH JOHN WHEAT

Foreword by Cactus Pryor
Introduction by Pat Culpepper

University of Texas Press ◄✦► AUSTIN

FRONTISPIECE: *On December 11, 1963, Darrell Royal accepts the MacArthur Bowl trophy for winning his first national championship. With Royal are General Douglas MacArthur (center) and UT Regent Wales Madden. Darrell K Royal Papers, Center for American History (hereafter CAH), DI01485.*

Requests for permission to reproduce material from this work should be sent to:
Permissions
University of Texas Press
P.O. Box 7819
Austin, TX 78713-7819
www.utexas.edu/utpress/about/bpermission.html

℗ The paper used in this book meets the minimum requirements of ANSI/NISO Z39.48-1992 (R1997) (Permanence of Paper).

LIBRARY OF CONGRESS CATALOGING-IN-PUBLICATION DATA
Royal, Darrell.
Coach Royal : conversations with a Texas football legend / Darrell Royal with John Wheat ; foreword by Cactus Pryor ; introduction by Pat Culpepper.— 1st ed.
        p.   cm. — (Voices and memories)
ISBN 0-292-70983-8 (cloth : alk. paper)
1. Royal, Darrell—Interviews. 2. Football coaches—United States—Interviews.
3. Texas Longhorns (Football team)—History. I. Wheat, John. II. Title. III. Series.
GV939.R69R69 2005
796.332′092—dc22   2005006652

Contents

Foreword

CACTUS PRYOR

Texas lost another one to Oklahoma when Darrell Royal was born a Sooner. But the University of Texas fixed that in December 1956 when Royal signed on as head football coach of the Texas Longhorns.

I had the pleasure to co-host Coach Royal's syndicated weekly television show for a number of years. My timing was perfect. I signed on just before the wishbone came to Austin. I was not a football journalist. I was a fan. One of the first sounds I heard in my life was the cheers riding the southern wind to our home a half mile north of Memorial Stadium.

So when I was offered the television opportunity I was delightfully shocked. The philosophy behind the station's choice was that a typical fan would ask the questions that John and Jane Doe would, not the deep stuff into which professional journalists would delve.

Every day I had watched the Longhorn workouts, from the era of Coach Clyde Littlefield to that of Dana X. Bible. My heroes ranged from Bobby Layne to "Spot" Collins to Noble Doss to James Street. Now I could add Darrell Royal, even before he coached a UT game. I sensed it. He looked right. He said the right things. He had the right chin. His accent was Texan. He had a sense of humor like Will Rogers's. At our first meeting I was in awe of the man, but soon I felt comfortable with him. He's down-home, and he out-married himself! And, what the heck! I was one year his elder.

Every Sunday at 8 A.M. during the season, we would gather in Lady Bird Johnson's television station in Austin to tape the *Darrell Royal Show*. Often we dragged ourselves into the studio. Some of the out-of-state games often meant very little, if any, sleep before taping. There was little rehearsing. We might decide what topics to discuss and I'd throw 'em and the coach would hit 'em. Of course we showed and discussed the game highlight films. And we'd usually have a pre-film feature that the producer had prepared. One that the coach suggested was a film of Mrs. Campbell working in her flower garden in Tyler,

Texas, talking about Earl and his brothers and sisters. Another of DKR's suggestions was an interview with a blind man who never missed a game in Memorial Stadium. It was a wonderful feature on a remarkable, happy man who saw the games with his ears and his accompanying friends.

A Texas newspaper wrote a feature about Darrell's good taste in clothes. The coach, who went barefoot during most of the Depression, did enjoy being able to dress for the occasion. I read the article on camera to Darrell. I should explain that, on Sunday mornings when we finished the shooting of the show, Royal would head straight over to the stadium to view with his coaches the entire film of the previous day's game, and I would head straight for the fields to train my Labrador retrievers. After reading the article to Darrell and the TV audience, I said, "Let's step out in front of our desk." Dutifully he consented. The television audience was treated to the sight of the coach's sloppy, grass-stained workout pants and tennis shoes that must have gone through World War II. They also saw my blue jeans splashed with mud and ventilated with several rips, plus boots dating from another generation. I then reread the news story about the natty coach. Royal responded with, "Well, you ain't Clark Gable yourself."

Darrell was President Lyndon Johnson's favorite football personality. After Johnson stepped down from the presidency he began attending University of Texas games. These were probably the only games he'd attended since his days at Southwest Texas State University. He would ask DKR to bring his players up to the LBJ Ranch on the Pedernales River for some barbecue, country music, and visiting. Several times Darrell, out of loyalty to the chief, shifted his schedule in order to accommodate LBJ's hospitality.

Once LBJ invited Darrell and Edith to join him and Mrs. Johnson for the Christmas holidays in Acapulco. During that vacation, when DKR was playing in a foursome with Bob Hope, former president of Mexico Miguel Alemán, and President Johnson, he was called on by LBJ to verify the correctness of a shot which Johnson had just made and which Hope and Alemán were questioning. Royal courageously agreed with Hope and the former Mexican president. For the rest of his life, LBJ would, with tongue in cheek, remind DKR of the day when he was not loyal to the president of the United States.

Royal was a master at handling a negative. Every Monday after the Saturday games he would face an auditorium full of tea-sippers waiting to hear his feelings about the game. One year, when the Texas Longhorns had been beaten yet again by the Sooners, the theater was running over. DKR faced the audience and began with typical Royal sincerity: "I didn't expect to see so many of you here today. Guess you wanted to see what the SOB was going to say about this one." The laughter signaled a touchdown.

I recall another such incident at the Headliners Club. This huge Austin club includes headline makers, newsmakers, Austin icons, and politicians. The entertainment is live, plus there are showings of films featuring goofs committed by the well-known during the preceding year. One year, after yet another defeat by Oklahoma, the auditorium was standing-room only. The crowd wanted to hear how Royal would handle this one.

The film showed me interviewing him in the usual post-game setting. My question to the coach was, "Darrell, we brought you down here to Texas to beat Oklahoma. Now we have suffered yet another defeat by the Sooners. What do you have to say about that?" The camera came in for a close-up of the coach's face. He spoke quietly and with great sincerity. "Well, I've done a lot of thinking about this situation. And I've turned to that famed scholar Oliver Wendell Holmes, who once said, 'As I look back on the days of my life I appreciated my defeats more than my victories, because I have learned more from my losses.' Well, I've been thinking about those words of that great man and I'd just like to say, 'Screw Oliver Wendell Holmes!'"

A five-minute side-splitter!

Coach Royal looked ahead. I shared a bedroom suite with him in a hotel in Rogers on the eve of the Game of the Century: Texas versus Arkansas. I would have slept better in a New York City bus. All night long the coach was calling his coaches in for yet another brain session. He didn't sleep a wink. In the morning, the buses waited to deliver the team to the stadium in Fayetteville. The players were very silent—even James Street, if you can believe it. Royal was the last to board the bus, only to turn around and disappear for a few minutes. I asked him what drew him back to the hotel. He explained that he had placed a call to a prospective hot high school recruit in a North Texas town. He wanted him to know that, even on this historic day, UT was thinking of him. (Incidentally, the guy signed with Oklahoma.)

And then there was the day when the hottest player in America, who was being sought by every college recruiter in the country, signed with Texas. Darrell went to visit with Ann Campbell. She welcomed him to their humble house. Coach Royal said, in essence, "Mrs. Campbell, we are here to tell you that we are offering Earl a good place to earn an education and the opportunity to make the Texas football team." Her response: "Coach Royal, you're the only one who said that Earl would have the OPPORTUNITY to make the team and to EARN an education. We're coming to Texas."

I've lived through over eight decades of UT coaches. I've seen them close-up, seen them adored and disliked. I've never seen one as admired and appreciated as Darrell K Royal. I doubt that our current football coach, Mack Brown, would have come to Texas had he not had the blessing of DKR.

Royal was the last major collegiate football coach to win a championship with an all-white team. He was the first coach to recruit a large number of extraordinary black players. He has continued to give to the University of Texas and to the city of Austin where he lives. There's hardly a good cause in Austin that doesn't bear his name, and he also gives to helpful causes throughout the nation. Edith Royal is side by side with her high school sweetheart. The Royals are our royalty in Texas.

Introduction

PAT CULPEPPER

Darrell Royal brought class and pride to the University of Texas football program and, because he was so successful, changed the perception that people had of the university itself.

Coach Royal was an energetic leader. During the 1960s he coached the Texas quarterbacks and was the driving force behind the Longhorn special-teams play. While I was at the university as a freshman in 1959, as a varsity player in 1960–1962, and as an assistant coach in 1963–1964, practices started during the season with Head Coach Royal tutoring the quarterbacks, backs, and receivers against the linebackers and secondary. He rehearsed the key plays he thought would make a difference in the upcoming game.

Coach Royal was a hands-on coach during those practices, but he did not baby his players. He came from a background where you pulled your own load. His desire to play football drove him to hitchhike back from California to his home in Hollis, Oklahoma, where he knew he would get his chance on the field. His inability to speak before large groups held him back as an assistant coach, so he memorized poems and turned his natural gift for observing human nature into a knack for saying the right thing at the right time, usually in a short and witty sentence.

Coach Royal cultivated a close friendship with the media and instituted informal post-game sessions at the Villa Capri Motel next to I-35, where food, drink, and conversation forged a strong bond between the coach and the writers from far and wide who had come to report on the games. Royal didn't make excuses when the Longhorns lost, and he was gracious in victory. He could have named the scores of countless games over his twenty-year stay at Texas, but that wasn't his style.

After cracking the strong hold his alma mater, Oklahoma, had over the Longhorns, Coach Royal not only brought the university three national championships, he also developed a football program at Texas without a hint of recruiting violations. During the late 1950s and early 1960s, Texas footballers, unlike those at other Southwest Conference schools, were required to take the SAT during their recruiting visits. In addition, professors from the Ivy League were being hired to change the academic environment on campus. Coach Royal met these challenges by hiring a "brain coach," requiring his athletes to attend every class, and inviting professors to pre-game preparations so that they could appreciate the efforts made by the Longhorn football program. Many of them became admirers of Royal's organization and his ability to communicate.

If you played football for Darrell Royal, you knew the kicking rules, you knew better than to draw stupid penalties, you understood the concept of playing as a team, and you were treated with respect by the coaching staff. When I became an assistant coach myself, I watched Royal go against Alabama's great Bear Bryant and pull off a 21–17 Orange Bowl victory in 1964. (Coach Royal continued to help me advance my career by calling administrators, time and time again, to help me get coaching jobs; through his influence, I secured my first head coaching job in a high school in Midland, Texas.)

I saw Coach Royal take time to give his pocket change to shoeshine boys in Dallas because he had worked at the same job as a youngster in Oklahoma City. And on a cold day in Amarillo, Texas, while I was with him on a recruiting trip, he told me, "It's how you treat the people who can't help you that counts." But in his years at Texas there would be friendships with the rich and famous as well, from President Lyndon Johnson to country singer Willie Nelson. Royal got a privileged view of the workings of America's highest office, and he also got to play chess with an outlaw singer.

Whatever the University of Texas football program is today is a direct result of Darrell Royal's insistence on doing things the right way. His story is important to understand because it is the very foundation for change at the University of Texas. His legacy became the standard to match for every football coach who followed his twenty-year tenure.

Nowadays Coach Royal is available to his ex-players and never forgets their contributions, and they, in turn, never forget the pride he took in them and showed them on a daily basis. His friends are better for their association with him. Coach Royal is a Texas treasure. He taught us how to win with class and how to get back to work when we lost. His generation experienced despair and hardship, saw the times change with desegregation, and witnessed the advent of illegal recruiting on a large scale in the 1970s. But Coach Royal never wavered in his principles. He was first my coach, then my friend, and I love him for who he is.

Note on the Interviews

JOHN WHEAT

I began my conversations with Coach Royal in the spring of 1993 to record in his own words the story of his legendary career at the University of Texas. I was eager to embrace this project because I had run on the UT track and cross-country teams in the early 1960s, and knew many of the personalities and events from Coach Royal's era. We sat down in the quietest corner we could find at the Barton Creek Country Club: in the wine cellar, surrounded by a thousand bottles of vintage wine.

As head of sound archives at the university's Center for American History, I intended merely to add the tapes and transcripts to the center's growing collection of Darrell Royal papers. The project took on a new dimension ten years later, however, when editors at the University of Texas Press read the transcripts and saw in them the potential for a fascinating book. To that end, I revisited Coach Royal (again in the wine cellar) in the summer of 2004, on the eve of his eightieth birthday, to update his story. Our conversations were all brought together and arranged under different topics. Although they do not include every anecdote from Coach Royal's fabled career, these conversations paint a compelling self-portrait of one of the most honored figures in the history of the University of Texas.

The Interviews

Growing Up

JW: *Coach, trace your boyhood in Hollis, Oklahoma, and tell us something about your upbringing and your experiences on up through high school.*

DR: This is a poor boy's story. I was born in 1924. My mother died when I was four months old, so I never had a mother. My dad moved into my grandparents' [house] for a while, until I was about five years old, and then he built a little house there in Hollis, Oklahoma, my hometown. Before I started grade school, my dad had built a new house.

Ever since I can remember, from the earliest time, I was just consumed with athletics. I had a brother, Glenn, who was four years older than me. Glenn and I would use Clabber Girl baking powder cans as our footballs. This was when I was a little bitty kid. I remember catching that can. Sometimes it'd hit on your finger or hit on the side. [laughs] But that was my first recollection of trying to do anything with football.

During the Dust Bowl days, the road right next to us wasn't paved, and it had just silt—it was like powder. And I remember drawing lines, and I had a stake, a piece of wood in the ground that I'd jump from. And I'd run and jump, and then I'd move the stake and make like a broad jump. I used to go down to the highway, which was only a block from us, and a car would be coming fairly soon, and I'd pick out a sign, and I'd try to get to that sign before the car did. I'd get a jump, and I'd try to gauge that so it was a good, tight race.

I'd do all kinds of things to compete by myself, just learning to do it a little faster and a little better. Then, I remember, one Christmas we got a rubber football. And that's when I first started trying to kick and throw a regular football, although it was rubber. And that rubber football was the best present I ever remember receiving as a little kid. Then I went on to grade school. Every recess we had some type of athletic contest, usually football—little kids' football, like we used to play in the yard. I remember playing on Saturdays with one of my buddies, Don Fox; we'd play in his yard, and we'd have maybe four or five guys that would play on Saturdays, and we'd put a radio outside and plug it in on the porch when the University of Oklahoma was playing. Of course, the band would play "Boomer Sooner" at different times, and I always felt like I was playing for the University of Oklahoma when I was running out there in the yard, playing in overalls. So it was always a big, big part of my life, as far back as I can remember. I was able to play junior high and, of course, high school football, and went on from there.

JW: *Did you live in Hollis all this time?*

DR: I lived in Hollis most of that time. I was only gone one summer. That was, as I said, back in the Dust Bowl days, and we lived by the highway. I remember watching those cars come by there, loaded down with furniture and those old canvas water bags that hung on the side of the car, headed west. They were all headed toward California. It wasn't long until we were in that line. I know my dad had an old Whippet, and he made a trailer. [Whippets, named for the racing dog, were a popular brand of car made by Willys-Overland in the 1920s and '30s.] Then we took what furniture we had in that old trailer, and got in that Whippet, and went to Porterville, California.

JW: *Where is Porterville?*

DR: Porterville is in the San Joaquin Valley. It's fairly close to Fresno. I got there, and I talked to the high-school football coach during the summer. I was small. I was even small when I was in college, but I was always small. And I talked to the high school coach, and I learned that they had teams by weight. You had to be a certain size to play with the big guys. That was the team that people cared about. They had those other teams just so little kids could play. I quizzed him about it: Could I try out for the larger team? He said, "No, if you don't weigh enough, you can't compete. You have to play on another team."

So I talked to my dad. I didn't like that idea, so I hitchhiked back to Hollis, Oklahoma, lived with my grandmother, worked my way through high school, and played high school football at Hollis, Oklahoma.

JW: *Were you also probably working in California?*

DR: Well, we did the normal things that you do when you go out there and look for jobs. We picked fruit. I remember painting figs with olive oil. They'd give you a jar of olive oil around your neck, and you'd climb up the ladder with

Darrell K Royal, Hollis, Oklahoma, ca. 1932.
Darrell K Royal Papers, CAH, DI01482.

Royal in his Hollis (OK) High School football uniform, 1942.
Darrell K Royal Papers, CAH, DI01569.

a paintbrush and dip it in there and touch the ends of those figs—cause 'em to ripen faster, get 'em to the market quicker. And just any kind of work like that that we could find. I worked construction. I found a job in construction pushing a wheelbarrow loaded with cement, and I would pour it into the forms. We did just any kind of work we could find. But I didn't stay there, except that one summer. I hitchhiked on back home.

JW: *Did you experience any of the kind of discrimination that a lot of the so-called Okies experienced in California?*

DR: Sure. And it affected me. If I think about it, I can still get kind of peeved. "Okie" was really a bad term. I appeared at halftime of the nationally televised Texas-Oklahoma game a few years ago. Bo Schembechler was doing color for the game, and Texas was ahead. Oklahoma started to get a little bit of a rally, and I said, "Hey, we better watch out. These Okies are getting stirred up." Well, I got a hot letter from a doctor from California, downgrading me and saying what an ungrateful Oklahoman I was and what a turncoat I was to turn on my Oklahoma upbringing and refer to Oklahomans as Okies. Well, he's still out there, and I guess he's still scarred by it.

But back then it was extremely derogatory, and it hurt to be called an Okie. But I overcame that a long, long time ago. The first big thing to happen to Oklahoma was the stage play *Oklahoma!* And then, of course, we had some success at the University of Oklahoma while I was there. We won our last twenty-one ball games. Then they won ten after that. So, that was a pride thing, and Okies became just a term. I lost that stigma back when I was a little kid.

But I wrote this guy back and I said, "Apparently you've never heard Merle Haggard's song 'I'm Proud to Be an Okie from Muskogee.'" And I said, "Everybody in Oklahoma that I've seen sing it is really proud of it, and I'm proud to be an Okie from Hollis, Oklahoma," and signed my name and sent it back to him. [laughs] I used the word "Okie" right back again. They say, "You're from Oklahoma." I say, "Yeah, I'm an Okie." But now people have forgotten *The Grapes of Wrath* and forgotten the Okie deal. That's a long answer to a very short question.

JW: *But you ran into it yourself.*

DR: Oh, absolutely, absolutely. I'm sure it's not unlike any minority person with those tags that they get. I can somehow relate to that and know how deeply they're cut by those tags.

Royal (left) and friends on air force duty in Florida, 1943. University of Oklahoma yearbook. Darrell K Royal Papers, CAH, CN09407.

Darrell Royal, from the University of Oklahoma yearbook, ca. late 1940s. Darrell K Royal Papers, CAH, CN09394.

JW: *And this case was probably a class discrimination. You were workers, and you were from somewhere else.*

DR: Oh, that's it, that's it. I've always had an Oklahoma drawl, southwest Oklahoma, and it used to be a lot worse than it is now. And they could spot you just right off, you know. I was a sophomore in college, I guess, before I found out I had a "finger" instead of a "fanger." I'm not proud of this, but I tried to change the way I talked. That one short summer out there I didn't want to talk like I was from Oklahoma, but I certainly got over that quickly, too. I'm from Oklahoma, I *am* from southwest Oklahoma, I'm proud of it.

JW: *Got to be what you are, right?*

DR: You got it.

JW: *So back in Hollis, then, you finished high school there?*

DR: Every day of my schooling, every single day, was in Oklahoma. Through high school it was in Hollis, Oklahoma, and then I went to the University of Oklahoma.

JW: *Of course you were already destined to go to the University of Oklahoma, I suppose, from this identification with it at the football games?*

DR: All I needed was an offer. [laughs]

JW: *Did you have a scholarship?*

DR: Oh yeah. I went right into World War II after high school, and I played on a service football team. Plus, I'd done well in high school, and I'd had a scholarship offer straight out of high school. But then having played on a service football team, I got a lot more offers.

JW: *What was recruiting like when you were in high school, when the colleges came around?*

DR: Well, see, there was no NCAA, there really were no rules. There wasn't much to follow. I visited a number of schools when I got out of the service. But it wasn't the high-pressure recruiting, even close, then that it is now, and there were very few rules or guidelines. So people did pretty well what they wanted to back then. But we're talking about 1946. That was a long time ago.

JW: *They just sent their scouts out and found out who was good?*

DR: Yeah, they didn't recruit hard. I was heavily recruited, and people were involved in it. But I think I had a coach—and he was an assistant coach—come to my hometown one time and spend about thirty minutes with me, and that was it. Of course, I didn't have any trouble making my mind up. I knew where I wanted to go to school.

JW: *What was the University of Oklahoma like? Were you strong academically there?*

DR: No, I never have been strong academically. I have been an average, and sometimes less-than-average, student. It seems like most of my academics was doing just enough so that someday I could go coach.

JW: *You knew that you wanted to be a coach all along?*

DR: Oh yeah, ever since I was in grade school and junior high. I knew that someday I wanted to be a coach. I'm not proud of this fact. I think I could've been a good student, but I wasn't. I wasn't academically motivated. I think probably the best single course I had in college, the one that I *know* helped me the most, was a class in business communications, which included letter writing. I still follow those policies today when I write letters. And when I read letters, it just flashes out to me when the writer of that letter doesn't adhere to those concepts.

Early Days of Football

JW: *Who was the head coach at the time you went to Oklahoma?*

DR: Jim Tatum was the head coach. He was there only one year, and left and went to Maryland. Coach Bud Wilkinson was the backfield coach, and he was my coach, actually. And then he became head coach, and he continued to instruct the quarterbacks and the offensive backfield. So, he was my coach all the way through.

JW: *What was he like, as a coach and as a person?*

DR: He was an excellent teacher. He wasn't a driving personality; he didn't jump on people. He was very patient; he was articulate. He thought he wanted to be an English professor, and he got into coaching kind of by accident. He expressed himself well, which made him a good teacher. You know, it really doesn't matter how many football plays you try to teach, it really doesn't matter how much you know, it's how much you can impart. And there are a lot of excellent football coaches who just can't impart the knowledge of what they want to get done clearly enough that the players can understand it.

I've heard of these highly sophisticated, complicated systems. I don't understand that. If it's that highly sophisticated and that complicated, I don't think the guys that are playing could play. You have to understand *clearly* what you're trying to accomplish, and that's what Coach Wilkinson did so well. It was so simple and so direct, and he expressed it so clearly and so well, that he was able to get players to do what he wanted them to do.

JW: *Did he become something of a role model for you when you thought about coaching?*

DR: Oh, I think I was influenced more by Coach Wilkinson than any other one single coach. I used the same approach, the same ideas, the same theory in

Bud Wilkinson
about 1963

Royal (right) with his coaching mentor Bud Wilkinson (left) and Des Moines Register
sportswriter Maury White, 1963. Darrell K Royal Papers, CAH, DI01547b.

coaching offenses. Now we changed our offenses, but I never did change the theory. I never did change the thoughts and the beliefs that I had, the way offensive
football should be played. And that was learned from Coach Wilkinson. I just
made a point not to try to copy his personality. I knew better than that. I had
to be myself: I had to do it the natural way for me and take a natural approach.
To the last day I coached, I stayed pretty much with the same theory that was
taught to me by Coach Wilkinson.

JW: *What sort of success did the Sooners have against the Texas Longhorns
while you were there?*

DR: Two and two. We lost our first two and won the next two. So as a
player, that was fifty-fifty. But the first victory was a big one. I think it broke an
eight-year drought. I think Texas had won eight in a row when we won in 1948.
I'm not sure about that, but I think that's the way it was. [Texas won the eight
match-ups from 1940 to 1947; Oklahoma triumphed in nine of the next ten.]

OU quarterback Royal being tackled by a defender after a six-yard gain in the annual UT-Oklahoma game, 1949. Prints and Photographs Collection, CAH, DI01548.

JW: *What did you know about the University of Texas? What sort of image did it have during that time?*

DR: See, I grew up six miles from the Red River and four miles from the Texas Panhandle. Our newspaper was a Wichita Falls paper, except for our little weekly paper we had there. So I knew about Texas football when I was a kid. And then having competed against them, I had the greatest respect for, and was always in awe, really, of the University of Texas. After I got into the coaching profession, I followed closely what was going on here. It's a strange thing. I used to daydream about what it'd be like to have a chance to coach at Texas.

I remember I was coaching at Mississippi State, and there was a coaching clinic in the state of Texas for the high school coaches, and then they had a high school all-star game. They would invite people back then to come and lecture at the clinic and then coach one of the squads. This particular all-star game that I worked in as a young head coach at Mississippi State was over in San Antonio. After the game was over, Edith, my wife, and I headed back to Mississippi. We detoured a little and came through Austin. And I just wanted to drive around the campus and circle the stadium and look at it. I'd never seen it. We always played the Texas-Oklahoma game in Dallas, so I hadn't been here. I'd never seen it. And, I remember—I remember *very* well—circling that stadium and looking at it and thinking how great it would be someday to have a chance to coach here. And circumstances fell so that, sure enough, I did wind up here.

JW: *That visit you're talking about would've been in the early '50s, then?*

DR: It would've been in 1954 or 1955.

JW: *You just mentioned your wife, Edith. We should get her in the picture. Where did you meet and when did you marry?*

DR: I met Edith when I was a junior in high school. She attended school in a little town by the name of Gould. It was eight miles from Hollis, but she was visiting a girl who was a classmate of mine. She was there spending the weekend with the girl. I met Edith at that time, and we started dating, and that was pretty much it. We knew pretty well that we were going to get married someday. And we talked about it, and then I went into the service. I'd been in the service a year and a half, something like that, when we married.

Becoming a
Football Coach

JW: *Would you briefly trace your coaching experience after you graduated from the University of Oklahoma.*

DR: I bounced around quite a bit. I always thought that it would be great if I could get a good high-school coaching job. That's what I thought I would be. And when I graduated from the University of Oklahoma—I graduated at midterm, after the 1949 season—I was contacted by El Reno High School. I went over and visited with them and did accept the coaching job. And that gave me a *little* bit of encouragement that maybe I could get a job at the college level. So I had an agreement with their superintendent who hired me, Mr. Taylor, that I would take the job. There was no team to coach. I went over there at midterm and started to work. And I said, "If I get a coaching job in college before June, I'll be free to leave. If I don't get a job by June, I'm here. I'm not going to leave after June, because it will be too late for them to hire another coach who could be there in time to coach the football team in the fall."

So I drew two paychecks from El Reno High School, and North Carolina State called me. Beattie Feathers was the coach at North Carolina State at that time, and he wanted me to be the freshman backfield coach. They were going to put in the split-T formation with our freshmen. And then the next year the varsity would use the split-T, and then I was going to be varsity backfield coach.

Well, I coached the freshman backfield for one year, and then I got a call from the University of Tulsa. Buddy Brothers was the head coach there. I got the varsity-backfield coaching job at the University of Tulsa. It was a pretty good boost in pay. We had a good year.

I stayed there one year, and I got a call from Murray Warmath, who was coaching at Mississippi State. So I went to Mississippi State. I felt like that was a move up, because Tulsa was in the Missouri Valley Conference, and Mississippi State was in the Southeastern Conference. I just felt it was a move up—not salary-wise, but professionally. I thought that would be a better move. Warmath

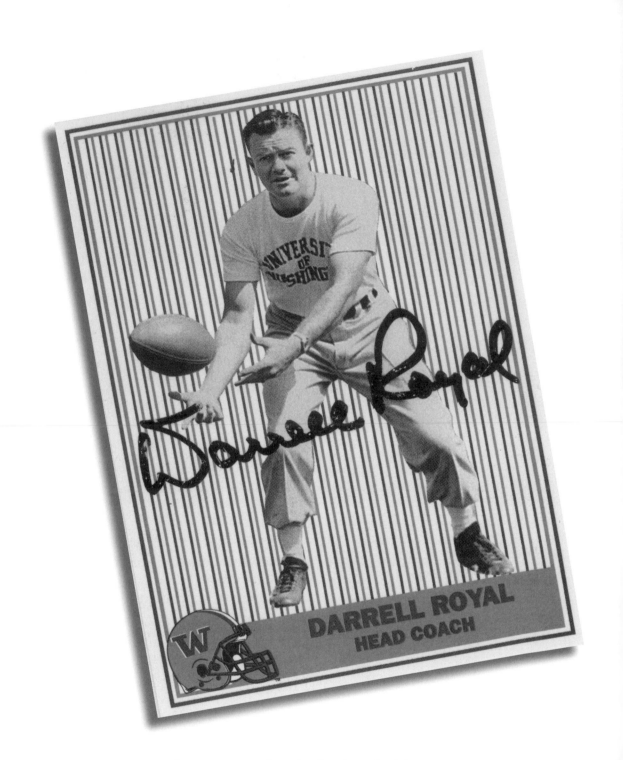

Royal spent one year (1955) as head coach of the University of Washington's football team, before becoming the head coach at UT. Prints and Photographs Collection, CAH, DI01549.

was a University of Tennessee man, and I wanted to learn more about the Tennessee philosophy, which helped me greatly, I might add. I stayed there one year. I was just really bouncing around.

I got a call from the Edmonton Eskimos in the Canadian professional league. I was twenty-seven years old. I went up and interviewed, and they offered me the job, and I took it. I coached there one year.

JW: *Were you the head coach?*

DR: I was the head coach. That was my first head-coaching job, and I was only three years out of college. I'd been to North Carolina State, Tulsa, and Mississippi State for one year each, as well as my two-month stay at El Reno. Murray Warmath left to go to the University of Minnesota. The athletic director at Mississippi State called me to come back from Canada to be the head coach at Mississippi State. I was twenty-eight. I took that job because in Canada there were only nine coaching jobs. And if you don't make it there, there's no place to go. There's not another job to fall into. And besides, I wanted to be in college coaching. So I coached at Mississippi State two years.

And then I got a call from the University of Washington in Seattle, and I went out there and coached one year. Then I got a call from Texas. Now I'd already established a reputation as being unstable, not knowing what I wanted to do or where I wanted to go. I remember Jack Gallagher, the sports writer in Houston, wrote in the *Houston Post* that I was "the peripatetic Darrell Royal." I called Jones Ramsey, the UT sports publicity director, and I said, "Jones, what is Jack saying about me here?" I said, "Is this bad or what?" I didn't know what the hell "peripatetic" was.

JW: *[laughs]*

DR: Jones said, "Oh, he says he means you move around a lot." I said, "Well, he's sure as hell right about that. He's nailed me on that, but he was talking like I won't be here long. I'm probably going to be moving and going somewhere else." But I knew quickly that the University of Texas was it. I had had a dream of this, as I told you earlier. I knew that I'd hit a spot where if I was ever going to do it, this is where I had just as good a chance as anywhere in the United States.

So I immediately set about my work. I never considered moving. I had numerous opportunities; I had numerous calls. I never even let people make an offer to me. I had calls from professional teams; I had calls from other colleges; I had calls from the University of Oklahoma twice. But I never even let it advance to the stage of hearing an offer, because even if it was a bigger financial offer, I would not have moved. I knew I was going to stay right here.

Edith and Darrell Royal at a Dallas Texas Exes gathering, 1966.
Darrell K Royal Papers, CAH, DI01550.

Coming to Texas

JW: *How was the initial contact made by UT?*

DR: I had told Edith about how great it would be to coach at Texas. Of course, she was with me when I circled the stadium in 1955 or 1954, whatever that year was. So we had talked about it. One night we were in bed and I got a phone call. I picked the phone up, and the voice on the other end said, "Darrell, this is D. X. Bible from the University of Texas." D. X. was the athletic director and former head coach. And I remember covering up the phone, and I said, "Edith, this is it." So they invited me to come for a visit.

I found out later that the University of Texas had a list of about 115 prospects, a list of everybody that they might be interested in talking to, and I didn't make the 115. The way I got the interview was that they called Duffy Daugherty [at Michigan State], who'd been contacted but had turned the job down. They called Bobby Dodd at Georgia Tech, who had been interviewed but had turned the job down. They called them separately. D. X. asked Duffy about a young coach, "somebody who's on the rise, somebody who you think maybe has potential." Duffy Daugherty gave my name. Bobby Dodd gave my name. Tonto Coleman, a West Texan, was working as assistant athletic director [at Georgia Tech] and was with Bobby Dodd. I was talking to Tonto Coleman from Washington all the time this Texas job was open because I knew that he was in on Bobby Dodd being interviewed. I *know* Tonto put in a good word with Bobby Dodd, and I knew Bobby. But it was kind of Tonto's influence that caused Bobby Dodd to recommend me, too.

Now, they didn't allow the two guys to get in cahoots with each other and pick a name. Mr. Bible called them separately, individually, and both of them gave my name. Mr. Bible said, "Well, heck, if both of them feel that way, let's call him and give him an interview." First of all, they told me to travel under an assumed name because they didn't want any more advance publicity. They had

had publicity on Duffy, they had had publicity on Bobby Dodd, and they had had publicity on Frank Leahy of Notre Dame. All kinds of stories were being spread about them coming to Texas. Mr. Bible wanted this to be handled differently. So he asked me to travel under an assumed name. I traveled under the name of Jim Pittman, who was my assistant coach at the University of Washington. [laughs]

JW: *[laughs]*

DR: I'd flown as far as Dallas, and I checked in as Jim Pittman there. And then I few to Austin and came into the old terminal at the airport, when it was a Quonset hut.

JW: *I remember that.*

DR: You know, it had the wire fence around it? And Mr. Bible was there to greet me, and he took me straight to the campus of the University of Texas.

JW: *This was in 1956?*

DR: 1956. Bible picked me up and took me immediately to the president's office. Logan Wilson was president at that time. He explained to me that we had academic standards, and we were going to adhere to those standards. And we were going to adhere to the rules. That didn't bother me. We had a quick interview. He then took me to the Athletics Council, and I visited with them.

Incidentally, I'd called Mr. Bible and said, "Who am I going to be interviewed by?" And he told me the order of it. I said, "Well, tell me who all's on the Athletics Council." And he said, well, so-and-so and so-and-so. I said, "Wait a minute, I mean the names." I wanted the names because I wanted to make sure I had everybody's name memorized and could refer to them as "John" or whatever. I remember Lloyd Hand was a student representative. I said, "How do I refer to these people?" He said, "Well, you can call so-and-so Dr. so-and-so. Myron Begeman, he's a professor, but he doesn't have a doctor's degree. You could refer to him as Mr. Begeman." I said, "How about Lloyd Hand?" He said, "He's a student. You can call him Lloyd." [laughs]

So, I had that all down pat. But anyway, we met with the Athletics Council, and then, after that interview was over, I was taken downtown to meet with the chairman of the board of regents, Tom Sealy, and some other members of the board at the old Commodore Perry Hotel. We were in a suite there. And then, after that interview was over, all of them got together, and they agreed to offer me the job. And I remember they met in a room and left me outside. Now with all this secrecy—traveling under an assumed name and all that—I was just

Dana X. Bible, head football coach (1937–1946) and athletic director at UT, who hired Royal as head coach in 1956. Prints and Photographs Collection, CAH, CN06906.

left out there, and this guy walked up to me and said, "Hi. I'm so-and-so." I said, "Pleased to meet you." He said, "And who are you?" I said, "Darrell Royal." It was in the president's office, so I said, "Darrell Royal." He said, "Thank you," and turned and—boom!—right out of there. He was an Associated Press writer. [laughs]

So they'd left me out there, and they already had it on the news before they got out of the meeting real good. But anyway, they offered me the job. The total process took less than five hours.

JW: *Really?*

DR: They said, "Well, what type salary do you think you ought to have?" I said, "I'm not going to be hard to get along with on salary." I said, "Just remember that this is going to be publicized. It's a matter of public record. Don't embarrass me or yourself. But I'll take the job."

JW: *What was the salary at that time?*

DR: $17,500. I was making $17,000 at the University of Washington. They bumped me a big total of $500 a year. And I coached about six years at that salary before I received a raise.

JW: *What sort of questions were they asking you when you met with the regents? What did they want to know?*

DR: I've forgotten. The only question I remember them asking me was what salary I thought I ought to have. And they asked me if I was interested in being athletic director. I said, "Well, yes, someday. Not now, I'm too young." I knew they wouldn't give it to me anyway. But I didn't want it. I was thirty-two years old. I didn't need the burden of being athletic director. I had a job to do; my hands were more than full just being coach. I said, "I would like to be considered for the position if, after I've been here a few years and my work proves satisfactory and you think that I'm qualified, you think I could handle the job. I would like to be considered for the athletic directorship." And unfortunately, Ed Olle, who'd been named athletic director, following Mr. Bible after his retirement, died of a sudden heart attack. I think I'd been here four years, something like that. I was named athletic director, too.

Coaching at Texas: The Early Years

JW: *At the time you came here—1956, starting in 1957—the University of Texas had been having a pretty tough time of it, with losing seasons. And there were high expectations that you were going to be able to turn this around.*

DR: Well, they were hopeful of that, but I felt that there was a lot of potential there. Normally when a squad only wins one game and loses nine, which is what Texas had done the year before, you find a totally bare cupboard, as far as football players are concerned. But Ed Price and his staff had recruited some really tough, hard-nosed freshmen. And, so we had that freshman class to build from, who would be sophomores the next fall, and we played a lot of sophomores. We started a lot of sophomores, and when those guys became seniors in 1959, we played in the Cotton Bowl against Syracuse.

So I started with a nucleus of a real good freshman class. Now the varsity players weren't that strong. But the freshman class that Ed Price and his staff had recruited was a darn good group of football players, and they were the ones who got us in the Cotton Bowl.

JW: *What was the atmosphere like here when you began coaching? What about the recruiting that you took over? What was it like by the time you began here?*

DR: Well, the University of Texas has always been able to recruit. One of the things that's hurting now is the high academic standards. It wasn't that high when I was working. But, let me back up and say what we first found. We found the facilities were really subpar. I was shocked at those facilities. The entire coaching staff was in one office. Now, I don't know how you can operate that way. The practice field had big ol' goat-head sticker burrs. Guys are not going to fall down and get with it in those goat-heads, I know that. You need a good place for them to practice.

JW: *Yeah.*

DR: So they practiced in the stadium a lot. And the coaching staff that I brought in here, they got to looking at these facilities and looking at the locker rooms and looking at office space, and they were really dejected and depressed over those facilities. I said, "Now wait a minute." I said, "What if we came in here and found everything top-notch, everything just like we wanted it, and the team just won one game last year, and everything was perfect here? What're we going to do to change? What are we going to do to turn the thing around? What are we going to do to improve it? All of these things can get done in time. I know the University of Texas is a first-class institution, and I think that I can sell the administration and sell the Athletics Council that these improvements need to be made for our program."

And I said, "You ought to be happy to find all these things because we can change all that. Now, they have a good freshman class here, so the University of Texas can still recruit. We can go recruit some more guys. If we get our facilities up, and we bring 'em in here, we can recruit even better."

So all of that was encouragement to me. Recruiting was very competitive. By then people were hiring full-time recruiters, and it was suggested to me that we hire a full-time recruiter. I got to analyzing the situation, and I found that we had a lot of players come in, but we weren't retaining 'em. And then I got to checking to see what the problem was. They were flunking out. So again I go back to the Athletics Council, and I say, "Look, we don't need a full-time recruiter. We need an academic adviser. We need somebody to help us *retain* these guys. We need somebody looking after the grades. I don't think coaches are good at that."

We'd always had the line coach take his players, and the backfield coach take his players, and the end coach take his players, and so on, and check on their academics. Well, they're football coaches. Besides, you're sending six or seven different people to talk to the same professors, and that wears out the professors, and *they* get mad.

JW: *Yeah.*

DR: I said, "We get one guy," and we found Lan Hewlett. He was recommended to me from Lockhart High School. He wasn't interested in being a football coach. We brought Lan Hewlett in as a counselor. And that's what I'm the most proud of, of anything that I did. We were the first school in the country that I have any knowledge of that hired a guy, full-time, as an academic coun-

*Royal looking
through his mail
at his office in
Gregory Gym,
1957. Darrell K
Royal Papers,
CAH, DI01507.*

*Royal conferring
with players Johnny Genung
(left) and Mike Cotton, 1961. Texas
Student Publications Photographs, CAH, DI01551.*

Lan Hewlett, 1968. Prints and Photographs Collection, CAH, CN07803.

Hewlett with assistant coach Charley Shira (left) and Tommy Ford (standing, right), ca. 1961. Darrell K Royal Papers, CAH, DI01552.

selor who was not a coach, not interested in *being* a coach. He was a teacher. And that thing has spread: there's not a single school in the country that doesn't have an academic counseling program now. The University of Texas has got an extremely sophisticated, high-dollar operation now. It's called the D. X. Bible Study Center. They've got three or four people working on the academics for the athletes, setting up tutors, and helping a player help himself—and this thing has spread all over the country. But we were the first to ever have it, here.

JW: *Is that right?*

DR: Yeah. As a matter of fact, there's a national award called the Lan Hewlett Award. They have a convention now, just like coaches have conventions. Academic counselors [gather from] all over the United States, and they present a Lan Hewlett Award at that national meeting every year.

JW: *When did he start working with you?*

DR: Nineteen fifty-seven.

JW: *Early on then.*

DR: Yeah.

JW: *How did you make contact with him?*

DR: One of the guys on the Athletics Council knew him. He said, "I've got a guy." I didn't know where to go. I had to get somebody to get recommendations. And he said, "I know a man over there that I think might be interested in the job. And if you're interested in talking to him, well, we'll get him over here." And he got him over, and I talked to Lan, and Lan took the job, and he started something that has just spread all over the United States.

JW: *How long did he work in that position?*

DR: Until just before I retired. I would say eighteen years. [Hewlett was in fact there twenty years, 1957–1977.]

JW: *I do remember him from my own track and cross-country days. He was also working with some members—scholarship people, especially—in track and cross-country.*

DR: That's right. And he just did it with one person. Of course, it's grown now. As I said, they've got a budget of about $500,000, I think, at the University of Texas now.

JW: *You had no trouble getting a salary and budgeting his position?*

DR: No. No.

JW: *They went for it immediately?*

DR: Immediately. They thought it was a good idea. I didn't have any trouble getting hardly anything, John, that made sense, you know? They were so supportive and so good to me, and I tried not to ask for things that were unreasonable. But I didn't have any trouble getting things okayed, no.

JW: *You, as you're suggesting, turned the team around, and it began having winning seasons and made it to the Cotton Bowl eventually. What sort of relationship did you have with alumni and booster groups at the time, in the '50s?*

DR: Apparently OK, because they didn't give me any problems. I made a lot of ex-students' meetings. Goodness knows how many March 2nd meetings I'd go to! They'd change the date. They'd say, "We won't have it on March 2nd. We'll have it, you know, another time," but they'd call them March 2nd meetings. I'd go to those, and I went to high school banquets, and I went to alumni meetings. I tried to visit and know the faculty, which is massive, as you know, when you take in the whole faculty.

But see, we got a good PR move in getting Lan Hewlett in here because he was the only one that was allowed to go talk to the faculty about athletes' grades or athletes' academic performance. And Lan had a great rapport with them because he was a teacher himself. So we had good rapport. I think I had good rapport with the administration. I always tried to stay 100 percent in the guidelines, in the chain of command. My guideline was to [report to] the athletic director. Then I became athletic director. Then my chain of command went to the Athletics Council, to the president, and to the regents. And when I wanted something, I didn't go to the regents and let it come back down. That makes everybody who it comes back down to mad—and when you lose, they will get your ass.

JW: *Right. [laughs]*

DR: [laughs] You're just better off staying in the chain of command, making requests, and letting things take the normal chain of command. Don't break the chain of command and go over somebody's head.

Royal paces the sidelines in this game in 1962. It was the last season that UT players' helmets had stripes. Texas Student Publications Photographs, CAH, DI01553.

COACH ROYAL ◀🏈▶ COACHING AT TEXAS

JW: *Did you?*

DR: I never was tempted to do that.

JW: *What sort of contact did you have then with the board of regents after you had started coaching?*

DR: I knew 'em all. And I was invited to their social functions, and I went to 'em. I knew who was on the board of regents. I knew who was going off the board of regents, and in many cases I knew who the governor was going to appoint *to* the board of regents. I made it a point to know those people. I made it a point to know the top administration over at the Tower. I made it a point to know the deans. And in many cases, the professors. I went to functions on the campus. Engineering would have a function, they'd invite me, and I'd go. I went to those faculty social functions.

JW: *In the first few years when you began, was there a tradition of inviting faculty members to accompany the team on the sidelines? When did that begin?*

DR: I think it was my first year here. We'd invite three faculty members as guest coaches. And all we did was bring them in, let them join us, and spend the day with us. I introduced 'em, and from that point on I didn't talk to them. I didn't visit with them, because I was busy. I was in preparation for the game, and I was totally focused, and I wasn't even aware they were on the sideline. They were invited right into the locker room before the game, to come in at halftime, to come in for the press conference if they wanted to, but I was busy doing something all the time. I couldn't play host. Lan Hewlett was with them, and *he* was their host. I just let them observe what we were doing.

JW: *That was the whole point of it, wasn't it?*

DR: Yeah. They saw me when I was pissed off, and they saw me when I was pleased, and they just saw me as I was out there. I didn't guard any of my emotions, any of my feelings. During the day, I didn't guard anything. "Here it is, you can see what we're doing, what we're teaching, what we're trying to accomplish. And you make up *your* mind what you think about our program."

JW: *Were you able to tell what kind of an impact that had on them?*

Royal at practice, with his "T" Association ring, ca. 1965. Photograph by Russell Lee. Darrell K Royal Papers, CAH, CN09397.

DR: I think it had a good effect.

JW: *On the Athletic Department and faculty relations?*

DR: Right. I think it did. They're still doing it.

JW: *Very interesting. I didn't realize how that had begun.*

DR: Well, I started giving "T" rings to the lettermen who graduated. I bought them personally so nobody could bitch about it. Later it became an Athletic Department expense, but when I started that program, I bought those rings myself. And I still see those rings. When I travel around the state of Texas, I see them from guys on the first squads that I coached.

Recruiting

JW: *What was the recruiting situation like when you had to go out and deal with high school players, say, by the late 1950s or early 1960s? How had things changed? You were describing a rather informal thing before.*

DR: Well, we had unlimited recruiting visits at that time. And our coaches would go to track meets all over the state. We'd go see guys time after time after time after time after time after time. Well, they've got some sanity in recruiting now. They've cut the length of time that you can recruit; they've cut the number of visits that you can go on; they've cut the number of visits that a prospect can make. He's got to boil it down and choose just x number of visits. They used to visit anywhere they wanted to visit, anywhere they were invited. So they've got some sanity in the rules of recruiting now.

JW: *So it was just a wide-open thing back in that era?*

DR: It's still highly competitive; I'm not saying that. It's more competitive all the time. Everything gets more competitive. I don't care what kind of rules they put in there.

JW: *When was the most intensive recruiting done? During the spring?*

DR: We recruited during the football season, during spring practice, during the spring and the summer. We recruited all the time because there was no limit on it. It was just year-round. And everybody knows that coaching has *some* input, but, boy, it's no substitute for material. You've got to have it.

JW: *There's been a long-standing feeling that, for example, the University of Oklahoma was recruiting a lot of the better players out of Texas. Was that the situation back in the '50s and early '60s?*

DR: They used to get a few out of the Panhandle from some of the schools that were closer to Norman than they are to Austin. But they expanded that, and they recruit all over the state now. But other people are recruiting all over the state. If you check Michigan, you find basketball and football players at Michigan, at Colorado, at Miami, at Florida State, at Oklahoma, at Nebraska—everywhere. Everybody's coming in and getting 'em. Used to be, we didn't lose except a few to Oklahoma and one or two to Notre Dame. Nobody else took any talent out of the state.

Racial Integration

JW: *What about the integration of athletics? In the early '60s the process of racial integration was just really beginning. There were no black athletic scholarships at the beginning. I think the very first black athletic scholarship may've been about '63, and it was not a football scholarship, it was a track scholarship.*

DR: Yes, James Means was the first black letterman in the Southwest Conference. SMU argues it's Jerry LeVias, but they're wrong. James Means lettered the semester before he did.

JW: *Tell me what was going on in the Athletic Department as they were addressing the whole question of scholarships and integrating teams.*

DR: Well, it was just a matter of time. And, of course, the proper thing—and the true feeling, too—is that we should've done it a lot sooner. But it wasn't done in this section of the country. No one did. I think all the schools integrated about the same time, within a year or two. Yeah, we didn't have integrated housing or integrated eating facilities. And you can take it even back from that to where they couldn't go in a restaurant or they had to go to a certain drinking fountain. They had their own drinking fountains. That had to change eventually and thank goodness it did.

But, you know, no one school is any more racist than the other, or any less racist than the other. They rap the University of Texas, saying it's more racist because they were the last to integrate, and that's not true. But that's recruiting talk; that's stuff that they put on you.

JW: *Were you able to convince black athletes eventually that the university was a good place for them to come to play football?*

DR: It was pretty hard. Now it's an accepted thing. See, back when I was coaching, you didn't see black families coming to the game. You didn't see black families wearing orange and white. You didn't see the little kids of the family with little Texas sweaters on. You just didn't see it. You didn't see blacks at the game. Well, obviously that's all changed. It's integrated and it's a thing of the past, thank goodness. Those kids have families, and just like everybody else, their families show up to the game, and they show up in support. And they're "hookin' 'em, Horns." That thing is disappearing about the University of Texas. Time has taken care of it.

JW: *Did you meet any resistance on the part of the university about integration of the team?*

DR: No. I was told that we didn't have it when I came here, but there was no resistance. No.

Once it started there was no resistance. I never was told, "Now, you can't do that." Except at first it was just understood. But I remember when I was a student at the University of Oklahoma; I remember the first black student who enrolled up there. They had a roped-off area for the black student to sit. Well, they say they're the big champion of integration. It wasn't that way when I was in school.

JW: *Yeah.*

DR: We're all of equal blame, and we're all of equal credit that we are integrated. One school is not more racist than another, and one school is not more considerate than the other. We're all about the same.

JW: *By about '64 you were athletic director. There was a question about the status of athletic director as a faculty position. What was the issue involved there?*

DR: Without my knowing anything about it, I was given a professorship.

JW: *Whose idea was that?*

DR: Dr. Ransom's.

JW: *This is Dr. Harry Ransom, who was the chancellor at the time.*

DR: And you know, I always said I'd never be a teacher and I'd never be a politician. And I look back on my twenty years, and I wasn't anything but both of them, full-time. Because, as I told you, I *knew* who was on the board of regents, and I knew who was going to go on the board of regents. I made it a point to find out as much as I could about that.

Teaching? Damn right, we were teachers. I was teaching, and I gave a test in front of 70,000 people every Saturday. We were teaching the game of foot-

Julius Whittier, UT's first black scholarship football letterman.
He played from 1970–1972. Prints and Photographs Collection, CAH, CN02060.

Royal at press conference in his new office in Belmont Hall, ca. 1972.
Darrell K. Royal Papers, CAH, DI01554.

ball. I would like to think that we taught it in an ethical way. I would like to think that we taught it in a sportsmanlike manner. I would like to think that we taught it to win. Important to win. Dad-blame right. Be no reason keeping records and keeping scores if it didn't matter. But I tried to make it truly a student-athlete situation. I detested people taking cheap shots. I didn't tolerate that. Encouraged and patted 'em on the back like you can't believe for a solid, head-on, jaw-to-jaw lick. It's a contact sport.

But there's a way to make contact, and there's a way that's totally unacceptable. The throwing of elbows and clipping—the things that cause injuries—I definitely was opposed to those things. And I taught that they're representing the University of Texas, whether they're on the field or not. Yeah, we taught a subject. I think I taught it well, so I don't apologize for that professorship. Some people it bothered.

JW: *Why did he do it?*

DR: I don't know. It gave me tenure. A full professorship comes with tenure. So in a sense it was security. But I never felt I *needed* security. I never used it. I never used it as a security measure, because we won enough that that was security. But it was an honor. It was a privilege that I was singled out for a distinct honor, and I consider it that. But I also don't take a backseat to the fact that I wasn't teaching something. I mean, I never wanted to be a teacher, I didn't want to teach in a classroom. When I said I'd never be a politician, I didn't want a political office. But you can't sit in Austin, Texas, and not know something about politics and not be politically in tune with what's going on at a state university.

JW: *Coach, let's talk about a few of the controversial things that people have written about you and about the UT football program. Of course there are always going to be some critics, so why don't we address some of those now, and then hear your side of the story. In 1972 a former player named Gary Shaw wrote a book called* Meat on the Hoof, *which is very critical of the program. What can you tell me about some of the things that he addressed in that book?*

DR: Well, I didn't read it for a long time, but I finally decided to read it. He had a couple of things in there about me, but, you know, that's his impression, and he's entitled to that. But what he said about me personally wasn't that bad, I didn't think. He indicted college football. He said he didn't even single out the University of Texas in particular. That this is just the way college football was, and he was opposed to that. That's the way he wound up his book. Now, he said a lot of things about our program. He wasn't talking about me personally, but he had a lot of things about our program that he didn't like, and he had some things in there that I didn't recognize.

Let me say this about Gary Shaw: he did not want to play football from junior high on. He says this in his book, that his dad forced him to play or encouraged him to play against his wishes. He didn't *want* to play. He didn't want to play high school football, and I know for a fact he didn't want to play college football. So picture yourself in his position: a guy out in uniform, and a coach pushing him and pressing him into doing some things that he doesn't like to do. It's a bad experience. He's *not* going to like the people that he's around.

I know one of the things he complained about was that we had two locker rooms. There were two small locker rooms, and we hadn't expanded at that time, so we *had* to have two. We had our freshmen and the lesser guys on the squad in one locker room and then the so-called playing squad in another locker room. And a guy would be promoted into the players' room or demoted back to the other room. He spent time in both locker rooms, and he didn't like either one of 'em. So we didn't have anything to please him.

JW: *Yeah.*

DR: I would say that 90 percent of that book that Gary wrote was expressing an honest view of a man who was out for a sport he didn't like. So naturally he didn't like anything we did. Now the most damaging was the 10 percent of it that is just absolutely not true. He had some drills in there, and some things that he *said* we did, that we just simply never did. That's goofy. No coach has things like that. You don't intentionally go out and eliminate your players through injury. It was the drills that he had in there that just simply did not exist.

JW: *What sort of reaction did you get when the book came out?*

DR: Well, I got a reaction because we were winning. That book wouldn't've been worth a continental damn if we hadn't been winning. And they put it out while we were on top and winning, and people read it and they commented on it. And I said basically to them what I've just said to you—that he gave an inaccurate report.

You know, I don't like to swim—I can't swim, I don't like to go underwater—and I would get an extreme dislike for a guy standing on the bank of a pool, blowing a whistle, telling me to jump in and get out, and then saying jump in again. No, I wouldn't like a guy who told me to keep jumping in and getting out. I might learn to swim after a while. Maybe it'd be good if somebody did that.

JW: *But you wouldn't necessarily like it.*

DR: No, I wouldn't like it.

JW: *Were you able to talk with him before the book came out?*

DR: No, I never talked to him. No.

JW: *Let's deal with the program as you ran it. What were some of the ways you would deal with players who you didn't feel were putting out their best effort? You said you considered yourself something of a disciplinarian, and you were hard. What was your typical practice approach?*

DR: Most players on the squad viewed it as a chance to improve, a chance to move up, a chance to earn a spot. Oh sure, it was as competitive as could be, and we listed our squads—how they rated—each day, whether they'd moved up or down, and that was posted. It was more prestigious, obviously, to be in the main locker room than it was the one in the back. That just worked out that way. Now we've got enough space to have everybody in the same room, and if I were coaching the squad today and had that large locker room, everybody'd stay in the same room. I separated 'em in any way, but that was a big motivation.

And I guess it *was* embarrassing for a kid to have to take all of his equipment, move out of the main locker room, and move back in the other locker room. But think what a badge of honor the other guy's wearing when he leaves the reserve locker room and moves in with the players. And it's a fact that the guys who are playing and the stars get more attention than the guys who are not.

But, I don't think we were unfair. Some of those drills were tough, but football is tough. It's a contact sport, and the only way you can learn to defend yourself and to play it properly is to have a lot of contact drills. As I said, most guys viewed it as a chance to learn a technique and learn how to play the game. I guess the best thing would be to interview some people who were on the squad at the same time Gary Shaw was. They have a totally different account of what we were doing. Totally. And they were interviewed. At that time a number of 'em went on talk shows and talked about it.

JW: *Shaw was particularly critical, as I recall, of Pat Culpepper as a coach, and fixed on personal characteristics of Pat—the way he spoke, for example.*

DR: It was more of an indictment of Pat Culpepper. He was a student assistant on the freshman team. Pat's an excellent football coach and doing very well. He has made the rounds in the coaching profession, and he's a dedicated football

Pat Culpepper, ca. 1962. UT Fleming University Writings Collection, CAH, DI01555.

man. He has no tolerance for people who don't give 100 percent. I mean, Pat's one of those unusual guys. Everything he saw about what we were doing, he was totally optimistic and totally full of it. I mean, he was right in the middle of it and competing and trying to earn a spot for himself—which he did, and started for us as a linebacker, even though he weighed only about 180 pounds. But they had two totally different mental approaches to the game of football.

JW: *So you managed to weather that little attack pretty well.*

DR: Weather it? It wasn't a factor. Not to me. I just went on about my job. It damn sure didn't cause me to alter anything I was doing.

JW: *When did you finally get around to reading the book?*

DR: Oh, reporters asked me about it. I think it was six months or so after the book was out that I got around to reading it, and I read every bit of it.

JW: *You mentioned that some of the players went on talk shows. That brings up the issue also of this sort of public-relations aspect of a coaching job and athletic director. Was there an interview program with the coach, you know, following Saturday games? Was it already instituted when you were here, or did you set that up yourself?*

DR: I think we expanded on it while I was here, but it always happened. Usually interviews were in the locker room. Every place I'd been, writers would come in immediately after the ball game, after you'd talked to the squad, and then you'd go meet with the press. I did that, and we also rented a suite over in the Villa Capri, an old motel that's torn down now. All the sportswriters would go over there after I'd showered and talked to the squad, and I'd go over there and sit and talk with them as long as they wanted to talk. Then I'd have another press conference on Monday, and then I had the Longhorn Club on Wednesdays, and I showed them the previous game film. So it was constant work relating with the press.

You know, I found out real early in coaching that I needed the press. I didn't need to fight the press. The press had a job to do, and I had a story to tell, so we needed to work together. I tried to work with the press. I tried my best on personal interviews to give a different train of thought, a different quote, so the reporter could write something different than what had already been written. I tried real hard to do that. And sometimes nothing came. But I tried, and I was thinking all the time to help a writer with the story when I was interviewed because, as I said, I had a story to tell and they had a job to do.

But reporters don't particularly care what a coach thinks or how he feels about football. Their editors tell them they have to write a story. So coaches get to thinking that the writers are just in awe of them. Oh, I think I have some great friends in the media. But, basically, when we were talking, we were working. They were doing their jobs and I was doing my job. We weren't just sitting down for a friendly chat.

JW: *But if you were providing them some good material for their story, then they're obviously going to feel good about you.*

DR: Sure.

JW: *They're not going to tend to come down on you.*

DR: That's right.

JW: *You also managed to come up with quite a few sort of folksy sayings over the years, and I think it was finally the object of a book that was put out about some of your quotable quotes. But you were also quoted in some newspaper stories as saying that you weren't really aware of their being all that colorful. It was just the way that you always spoke.*

DR: No, I guess probably the most quoted thing I told the press was that there are three things that can happen to you when you throw the football, and two of 'em are bad. The odds are against throwing, so why throw the ball? Well, I was kidding. That was tongue-in-cheek, and I was really kind of playing with 'em because we had a good running attack that year. Most of the years we were any good, we had a good running attack.

But we weren't throwing the ball, and they kept asking, "When're you going to throw the ball?" We were leading the nation in scoring one year, and still I would be asked, "When are you going to start throwing the ball?" I thought the object was to score, and we were leading the nation in scoring. Still they would ask, "What about your passing attack?" So I made that statement, just kind of playing with 'em. But I had no idea that that would go around the way it did.

JW: *And now it's sort of become a truism.*

Royal celebrates Billy Dale's two-yard touchdown run in UT's 21–17 win over Notre Dame in the 1970 Cotton Bowl. It was the football program's 500th win, and Royal's second national championship. Photograph by Linda Kaye. Prints and Photographs Collection, CAH, CN07537.

Cactus Pryor and Darrell Royal on the set of Royal's Sunday TV program, ca. 1970s. Darrell K Royal Papers, CAH, DI01513.

DR: Yeah, and people really and truly believe that I'm just anti-pass. Did you know in all the big football games, you can trace it back where the turning point was a pass thrown by us? The [1969] Arkansas game? The [1970] Notre Dame game?

JW: *Yeah, right.*

DR: When we played Joe Namath in Alabama, Bear Bryant was coaching 'em in the [1964] Orange Bowl. Just pick one—there's a pass in there. There're some crucial passes that made a big, big difference in the game.

JW: *And it works the other direction, too, doesn't it, or a pass thrown against you?*

DR: Oh, I never did care. I don't think it's derogatory that people thought that we were anti-pass, but we worked hard on our passing attack. We just didn't use it much, but when we did it was effective.

JW: *Yeah, then the other phrase: "three yards in a cloud of dust." I believe that was the other phrase.*

DR: Yeah. That's the way people described us, and I had nothing to do with that. I don't know where that came from; somebody else said that.

JW: *I guess your most famous quote is, of course, "You got to dance with who brung you." Was that a phrase from your daily life, from your upbringing?*

DR: Oh, there was an old song. You know, somebody sent me the song. It's an old sheet-music thing. I've got it framed at the house, and the song is called "Dance with Who Brung You." So, somewhere in my past I heard that. I don't know where. It came out when we were playing Notre Dame the first time, and they had us greatly outweighed. And we had a running attack, and we were in the wishbone, and some of the writers wanted to know if I was gonna change our attack. I said, "No, we're gonna dance with who brung us." And it was a throwback from something that I'd heard a long time ago. I was just saying we're gonna do the same thing. But you know, that's the way people talk pretty much in southwest Oklahoma and kind of the way I grew up.

JW: *Back to the issue of the public relations. You also eventually started doing a television show, usually the Sunday after a Saturday game, in which you'd have about a half hour to talk, usually with an interviewer. Didn't you start this?*

DR: Yes, Cactus Pryor and I did it for years.

JW: *Where did you first meet up with Cactus Pryor and start the relationship?*

DR: Of course it's hard to live in Austin, Texas, and not meet up with Cactus Pryor. All those great, great luncheons they used to have at the Headliners Club, and Cactus always emceed those. I was a member, and still am, of the Headliners Club, and I went to all those luncheons, and I was kind of material for Cactus. He'd razz me along with the people that were being honored at the Headliners Club. But Cactus and I are just really good friends. I'm very fond of him, and we did the TV show together for a number of years. It was a great experience, and Cactus and I still do things together.

JW: *Had there been a show like that before?*

DR: Oh yeah, I'm sure. I think just about every coach had a TV show. There wasn't anything new about that.

JW: *What did you try to accomplish on a typical program like that?*

DR: Well, hopefully, prospects watched those things some of the time. And maybe they would get to know you a little bit through that medium before you call on 'em. And their parents maybe have watched the TV show, and when you knock on their door to come talk to 'em about recruiting their son, you're not a total stranger—that's one thing. It gives a way to communicate with the alumni and the boosters and backers. It gives a chance to pat the guys on the back that actually were in the game, to point out their good plays. It's a chance for a little bit of side revenue for the coach.

JW: *[laughs]*

DR: It wasn't much. My last year, I think I made $3,500 out of my TV show. Now they make a bunch of money out of it. Of course, the price of a coach has gone up greatly since I quit.

Player Preparation

JW: *Let's talk a little bit about the one of the perennial issues, the use of steroids in the preparation for athletic competition. I understand it's been going on for a long time, but what sort of problem did you face, or how aware were you of it as a problem in your own program?*

DR: I just don't have a memory of it being a problem or being in existence. I think most of that stuff has come about since I resigned.

JW: *It's that recent?*

DR: Yeah, I've been out of it since 1976. So that's a thing that was just starting. People were starting to bulk up. But I wasn't aware of it. It wasn't a problem. I didn't know anything about it.

JW: *How much emphasis was put on weight training while you were running the program?*

DR: I, for one, never did feel that the weight training should be a big part. We had a great guy, Charlie Craven, who oversaw our weight program, and that was mainly for rehabilitation: knee injuries, shoulder injuries, leg injuries, to build 'em back up and strengthen the knee, strengthen the muscles to support the knee. We used it some in conditioning, but I never cared how much they could bench-press—I never cared how much they could lift—because I was going to judge them on how well they played football, not on how well they lifted weights. So I never did emphasize it.

Obviously, I was behind the times, because now everybody thinks it's just a vital part of the game, and it probably is. I felt the weight program was important, but we didn't stress it. It's a game of mobility. As long as they keep the field the length it is and the width it is, somebody's gonna have to run to play it. And I wasn't interested in a bunch of bulky and muscle-bound guys who couldn't get down and weren't agile.

JW: *Today, in particular, you see linemen who have huge necks and who have bulked up enormously. But I remember back on the '63 squad, Tommy Nobis, for example. Now he had a large neck and all that, but how much did he weigh? He was very agile, that's for sure.*

DR: Tommy weighed maybe 215.

JW: *That's very light by today's standards.*

DR: Yeah, I think he got up to about 240 or something like that in professional football. But the '63 squad was a light squad. People have just grown, whether they're in athletics or not. They're wearing larger shoes and they're just bigger. I don't know where it's gonna stop. But the size of linemen now is just mind-boggling.

JW: *I remember way back in the late '50s, around '60, Detroit had a lineman, Les Bingaman, who was a 300-pounder, and he was considered almost a freak out there. But nowadays you've got lots of 300-pounders.*

DR: A bunch of 'em. And they can move. Not only do they weigh a bunch, but they can move and get about. Yeah, it's changed.

JW: *But that was not your approach to it then.*

DR: Oh, I would've loved to've had those big guys who could run. But when you use weights just to bulk up and to be strong, but you make yourself less mobile, I wouldn't want that.

JW: *Talk me through a typical week's preparation for a big game. What would be the sequence of workouts on each day? Was there a standard routine that you would follow?*

DR: We got into one. It was pretty standard for us. Sundays we didn't do anything. We looked at the game film on Sunday afternoon or Sunday evening, and then Monday, the ones who played worked out in sweat clothes, and we scrimmaged those who didn't play. Then on Tuesday we worked two hours, in pads, pretty hard. On Wednesday we worked an hour and a half. Thursdays, a lot of times we'd be in sweat clothes and shorts, about an hour and fifteen minutes. Friday, we'd put on just sweats and go out and not even run enough to break a sweat. We'd kind of walk through some situations, walk through some substitutions, and talk about the bench and being alert when we're on goal-line defense or goal-line offense or special teams, and we'd go over that. And then Saturday

All-American Tommy Nobis, ca. 1963. Nobis went on to star with the NFL's Atlanta Falcons, where he played for ten seasons. In 1981 he was inducted into the College Football Hall of Fame. Prints and Photographs Collection, CAH, DI01556.

Royal on the sidelines during the UT-Arkansas game, 1965. Photograph © Time, Inc. Darrell K Royal Papers, CAH, DI01502.

Royal urging his team on from the sidelines, ca. 1965. Darrell K Royal Papers, CAH, DI01487.

we'd play the game, and then repeat it. But we didn't work a whole lot once the season got going. Our workouts were two hours maximum.

JW: *Standard practice would be you would always take the team somewhere away from their usual surroundings, would you not?*

DR: Yes, we did. We took 'em to a motel on Friday nights.

JW: *Even here in Austin?*

DR: Even when we were home, because it just gets 'em together and they're thinking, you know. It's part of the mental preparation. Too, it's getting 'em out of the dormitory, getting 'em away from people calling from their home-towns, coming in, wanting to come by and see 'em, and that type thing. It just kind of gets 'em isolated and gets their mind on the work at hand tomorrow.

JW: *Looking at another aspect of the way you coached, I've noticed a great deal of development in recent years, since your retirement, of communications. Talk about the problems of communicating in a loud, crowded stadium with the game pressures and time considerations running. How did you handle communication between yourself, your press-box people, your other coaches, and the players on the field? Sounds like a terrible problem to me.*

DR: Well, you know, strangely, I wasn't aware too much of the people in the stands. I knew that some games were extremely noisy, but I always had on a headset. And you know, that's a big earpiece, which blocks out a lot of that noise, and you can hear clearly the press box. I could talk to them. I don't care how loud it was, the headset muffled it out and we had easy communications. We used hand signals, like everybody else was doing at that time, to signal in information.

JW: *Who would you have in the press box?*

DR: I had the offensive backfield coach who I was talking to, and Mike Campbell had some of his defensive staff. Mike liked to operate from the side-line, and I did, too.

JW: *Did you have the earphone or headset when you came in 1957? Was that already around?*

DR: It wasn't. It grew, and got more sophisticated all the time. I remember, my first head-coaching job was in a Canadian professional league, and we had no press box to talk to and no communications there, just had a phone-type deal.

Earl Campbell's #20 jersey was retired in 1979. Here, Campbell, who was recruited by Royal to play for UT and who won the Heisman Trophy in 1977, speaks with his former coach. Darrell K Royal Papers, CAH, DI01557.

At Mississippi State I didn't wear a headset; I didn't wear a headset when I was coaching at the University of Washington. It started here, and communications between the staff have just gotten much more sophisticated than it was. We were a little bit simpler; we didn't have a very complicated way of doing things. Our defense wasn't that complicated, and our offense seldom consisted of more than six or seven—eight, maximum—running plays. Four to the right and four to the left, so basically it was a decision of whether you're gonna go right or whether you're gonna go left. And all of our plays were kind of short-yardage plays. Sometimes a great runner would have a pretty good hole, and he would break a long run. But actually when that play was called, we probably thought we'd make three, four, five yards.

JW: *You would consider it successful when you got that.*

DR: I would have, yes. Then a great runner—a Chris Gilbert or a James Saxton or Earl Campbell—would turn those three-yard runs into forty, sixty yards. And as the other team wears down, if you are superior, what starts out in the first quarter as two-, three-, five-yard gains becomes six, seven, ten, fifteen yards. I mean, those runs get bigger as it goes into the fourth quarter, when you start to dominate, if you're better. Of course, I've been in those ball games where, if you started out making nothing, you wound up making nothing, too. This game wasn't that complicated, and we were making all these changes.

The Wishbone

JW: *Did that have anything to do with the wishbone?*

DR: Totally different philosophy.

JW: *But what is the basis of the wishbone? What's the whole emphasis, by running that? First of all, just for the record, explain the wishbone formation.*

DR: Well, it's a triple option, to begin with. The quarterback reads the defensive tackle, and he gives the ball to the fullback if the tackle hasn't closed. But if the tackle closes down on the fullback, the quarterback takes it out and runs out to the end. At that point he's got another quick option. If the defensive end drifts, he keeps the ball. But if the defensive end takes him, he pitches it to the halfback trailing behind him. So when we'd call one play, it was actually three plays because it would either be a hand-off, a quarterback keep, or a pitch to the trailing halfback. So we didn't have to have a lot of plays.

JW: *The wishbone would be, I imagine, when the running backs are behind the quarterback in sort of a Y configuration?*

DR: Yeah. The way it got its name, we were in this offense for two games, and we were in this press conference I was telling you about over at the Villa Capri. Mickey Herskowitz, the writer from Houston, was there. And someone asked me, "What do you call this formation you're in?" I said, "We haven't called it anything. It's just the way we line up." He said, "Well, don't you think it ought to have a name? Are you going to stay with it?" I said, "We probably will." "Well, don't you think it ought to have a name?" I said, "Well, they're kind of in the shape of a Y back there. Call it the Y." I mean, I didn't care what they called it, you know. Mickey Herskowitz said, "That's not very original. Why don't you call it a wishbone? It's in the shape of a wishbone." I said, "You got it, Mickey. It's a wishbone."

JW: *That's where they coined the name?*

DR: Yeah. He named it. Mickey Herskowitz named it. We just lined up that way.

JW: *Now, that offense caught on, and a lot of teams were using that for years, to great effectiveness. But certain plans seem to run their course as defenses adjust to them. Did that happen to the wishbone?*

DR: People are still running it. There're a number of wishbone teams. I still see the wishbone. So people are still using it.

JW: *Sports commentators are always talking about how something has run its course.*

DR: Oh hell yes. And they talk about the wishbone, say that you can't come from behind, that it's not any good when you're behind with two minutes to go. My rebuttal to that is you're supposed to be doing something the first fifty-eight minutes. The object of your game is not be behind with two minutes to go. I've watched ball games and heard commentators say, "Wishbone will go behind by a touchdown." They say, "Well, you know, the wishbone's not an offense to come from behind."

I was watching Alabama play Auburn one time. Auburn got ahead 7–0. The first thing they said was, "Well, you know, the wishbone can't come . . ." They didn't get it out of their mouth good until Alabama scored, tied the ball game up. So now, Auburn scores again. Says, "Well, he's undaunted." They said, "Well, you know, the wishbone, it is hard to come from behind." And didn't get it out of his mouth good until Alabama scored again, came from behind, just— boom!—right quick. Alabama winds up winning the ball game. But I guarantee you that same announcer went to the next game, and if they were running the wishbone and if they ever got behind—"Well, you know, this wishbone is not a good offense to come from behind in."

We came from behind with six minutes to go against Notre Dame in the Cotton Bowl in a muddy field. We had six minutes to go and were seventy yards away. We were behind 14–0 in the ball game in 1969 against Arkansas. But I'm sure they were saying that in the booth: "Well, you know, this wishbone can't come from behind." We came from behind.

JW: *And as you pointed out, by a pass.*

DR: Yeah, well, you might remember the [1970] UCLA game here. We

Quarterback James Street and Royal confer before Street connects with Cotton Speyer on a critical fourth-down pass against Notre Dame in the 1970 Cotton Bowl. Photograph by Linda Kaye. Darrell K Royal Papers, CAH, CN11611.

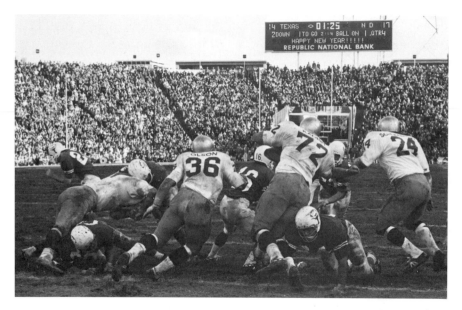

UT Guard Bobby Wuensch (on ground) seals off Notre Dame's defensive line, allowing Billy Dale to score the game-winning touchdown. Prints and Photographs Collection, CAH, CN07535.

were behind with nineteen seconds to go, and we were fifty-something yards away and had no time-outs. And we won it with a pass.

A lot of our big ball games were won throwing, but the wishbone was a good offense. I don't know whether it'd go in today's market or not. I don't care.

JW: *Is the wishbone something that you developed?*

DR: Emory Bellard came up with the idea. He was the backfield coach here then, and he came up with the alignment and the way we'd run it. We incorporated some of the things that I was taught under Bud Wilkinson at Oklahoma. Some of the same things were in that package, but Emory Bellard had the idea of the alignment. We had to modify it a little bit as we fooled with it and played some games. We had our fullback too tight to begin with, and we didn't realize it through scrimmages. But I called Emory one night after a ball game and said, "Emory, I think we'd be a lot more effective if we'd get that fullback back a little deeper." He said, "You know, I was just going to call you on that." He said, "I'd already had the idea"—so Emory and I thought a lot alike. I mean, it was amazing how we agreed on offensive strategy. But it was his idea. Mickey Herskowitz named it.

JW: *You had a great combination. Again, back to the question of communication, in situations like the famous Arkansas game in 1969, where you're down to a fourth down, a great deal of pressure, a great deal of national attention focused on the play, great drama, and your quarterback comes off the field and you've got to make a decision. What went into your decision about throwing the pass that, of course, ultimately did result in a touchdown?*

DR: Well, they'd had a confusing defense for us. They had a stunt that we couldn't solve that day. We hadn't had but one or two running plays over three yards all day. They had pretty well shut us down, and time was running out. And I felt that if we *did* run the ball and make a first down, that we probably would not have the ability to sustain the drive, because we hadn't been able to do it all day.

JW: *You were pretty far back on the field, weren't you?*

DR: We were, and I felt we had to get something big. It was time to really take the gamble. Of course, it was a perfect throw and a perfect catch. People

Legendary Notre Dame coach Ara Parseghian congratulates Royal after the Longhorns defeated the Fighting Irish in the 1970 Cotton Bowl. The scoreboard shows that UT had won the national championship. Darrell K Royal Papers, CAH, DI01504.

Royal on the sidelines leading his top-ranked Longhorns against second-ranked Arkansas on December 6, 1969, at Razorback Stadium.
Darrell K Royal Papers, CAH, DI01558.

COACH ROYAL ◀🏈▶ THE WISHBONE

The Longhorns' sideline erupts after James Street's 44-yard pass completion to Randy Peschel, Royal already is considering his next move. Two plays later, Jim Bertlesen scored from two yards out, tying the game at 14. Happy Feller kicked the extra point, giving UT a dramatic, come-from-behind victory. Darrell K Royal Papers, CAH, DI01503.

The scoreboard at Razorback Stadium tells the story of the Longhorns' stunning victory over Arkansas. Prints and Photographs Collection, CAH, DI01559 and DI01560.

Following the UT-Arkansas game, President Richard Nixon (at microphone) congratulates Royal, Street (behind Nixon), and linebacker Glen Halsell (behind Street). ABC reporter Bill Fleming (far left) captures the president's words for the national TV audience. Prints and Photographs Collection, CAH, CN01766.

talk about that being a brave call and a courageous call and a great call. If that pass had been incomplete, it'd been the most criticized call. They'd have said, "It's stupid as hell. They're not a passing team. Should've been running the ball, pick up the first down." But we weren't moving the ball that well. So I felt we had to gamble, had to go for it. We were behind. We had to do something.

JW: *Did that fall into the category of the "Hail Mary"? What kind of a play was that?*

DR: It wasn't the "Hail Mary"—it wasn't that. No, you've got to pick something. They give you twenty-five seconds to make up your mind and get it going, so you have to call something. Of course, my whole life was spent on those twenty-five-second decisions, and you get used to it. You just call something, and I felt that was what ran through my mind. Though by looking at that clock, there's about four minutes to go, and if we make first down, we can't score; we don't have enough time on the clock. The time would get us if we tried to make it in by running the ball. Plus, we'd not been able to keep a sustained drive going. So we had to do something else. We had to break the pattern, break the mold. We had to go a different direction.

And, I was hoping that it'd catch 'em by total surprise. I'll tell you how surprised they were. They had their safety men and their halfback all over Randy Peschel. I mean, he was as well covered as you could be covered. And when James Street threw the ball to Peschel, there were six hands going after the football, and all within probably six inches, maybe as little as an inch or two. And it happened to get in Peschel's hands, but the defensive people were all over the ball. One of them said that he thinks the ball grazed his fingertips as it went into Peschel's hand, so that's how close it was to being an *unsuccessful* play. And had it been unsuccessful, Lord knows they'd still be criticizing me.

JW: *Well, it was a moment of high drama. Of course, it was the centennial year of college football, and the game was for the national championship, so there was a great deal of attention focused on it. Of course, in the locker room afterward the president of the United States shows up to deliver the MacArthur Trophy.*

DR: No, that was President Nixon's personal trophy. You know, there were a bunch of other people there. George H. W. Bush was there. Henry Kissinger was there. H. R. Haldeman.

JW: *The White House staff?*

DR: The White House staff.

JW: *Yeah. Nixon was a very big fan. In fact, he used to use football analogies to talk about politics.*

DR: Yeah, that's right. But Billy Graham, I think I mentioned him, was there. But all those White House guys—Ehrlichman and Haldeman—all those guys were there. Who's the tough guy who burns himself?

JW: *[laughs] G. Gordon Liddy.*

DR: Gordon Liddy. [laughs]

Lyndon Johnson, Mance Lipscomb, and JFK

JW: *Well, this brings up an area of your association with a lot of really well-known people as a result of the attention that gets focused on the games, and one of the more obvious ones, of course, would probably be Lyndon Johnson. You were here when he was the Senate majority leader, and then he eventually became vice president and president. What sort of relationship did you develop with him?*

DR: Well, it grew over the years, and I really got to know President Johnson well after he was out of office. He had invited Edith and me to the White House, and we'd gone up. But after he came back to the ranch, he attended all of our home ball games, and he traveled out of town to our games. I used to take some of the guys on the squad out to the ranch to meet the president. We'd go out and have lunch with him. He enjoyed the game a lot more when he knew some of the players personally, and that is the reason I did it.

President Johnson enjoyed the excitement of the crowd. He was a football fan, but he knew what drew interest and what drew crowds. I'd seen him go to country music concerts. And he'd look around at the crowd, their reaction to the entertainer up there, and he was enjoying the entertainer at the same time. I remember calling Charley Pride, and I said, "Charley, why don't you call President Johnson and invite him to your concert tonight?" He said, "Oh, I can't do that! I can't do that!" I said, "Sure, you can. Here's his number—call him." And sure enough, President Johnson went to the concert. And I was seated right behind him, and that's when I noticed him. He watched the crowd a lot and their reactions, and then he enjoyed the performance on the stage, too. He knew what stirred up excitement, what caused people to be enthused, and I think that intrigued him about as much as the game.

The last two years of his life, my wife and I vacationed with him and Mrs. Johnson in Acapulco. We were scheduled to go on the third trip when, a week later, he had his fatal heart attack. We'd take our grandkids out to the ranch,

Royal in conversation with Vice President Lyndon Johnson and his wife Lady Bird at a Texas Exes' celebration, January 1, 1962. Darrell K Royal Papers, CAH, DI01533.

STONEWALL, TEXAS

Dear Darrell:

I am very grateful to you and the Band and
everybody else for the courtesies shown me
Saturday night.

Especially, I want you and the team to know
how much I enjoyed seeing the fine way in
which they handled themselves on the football
field. I know you are proud of them and I am
too. They are a great group of young fellows
and you are the finest example of an inspiring
and worthy leader I know.

With best wishes to all of you.

Sincerely,

Mr. Darrell Royal
Director of Athletics
University of Texas
Austin, Texas

October 7, 1969

P.S. We must get together with our wives soon.

*Royal's longtime friendship with LBJ is captured in this letter from the former president
in October 1969. Darrell K Royal Papers, CAH, DI01529.*

Royal, Lady Bird Johnson, and Lyndon Johnson enjoy the music at the Kerrville Folk Festival in 1972. This photograph originally appeared in the Kerrville Daily Times. *Rod Kennedy Presents, Inc. Archives, CAH, DI01574.*

and I'd play golf with him. We played golf; what little golf he played, I think, I must've been involved in all those games. I know one time Tom Frost and I played golf in Acapulco with Gustavo Díaz Ordaz and President Johnson. Tom Frost is the banker from San Antonio. There was a little bit of a speech barrier, but we all understood the game of golf. President Johnson won it on the last hole. [laughs] So he beat Díaz Ordaz, and Díaz Ordaz paid off in pesos. I don't know how many. It was a small amount of pesos—about a dollar, or something like that.

JW: *And what about Mance Lipscomb, the great singer-guitarist? One of the places that he appeared was at the first Kerrville Folk Festival, in 1972, and there's a newspaper photo from the Kerrville paper that shows President Johnson and Lady Bird, with you in the foreground, at that Kerrville concert. Was there anybody in particular that the president wanted to see?*

DR: Well, I'll tell you the way that came about. Edith was out at the ranch, and President Johnson told her, "If you'll tell Darrell, he'll come over, and we'll play golf in the afternoon, and then I'll go with him to listen to his pickers." Now, that's the way he referred to it. Now, [laughs] they're not my pickers. They're friends of mine. That's really what he was saying and what he meant.

After we walked in and were seated, Kenneth Threadgill was the first one up. He played the old Jimmie Rodgers tune "All Around the Water Tank": "All around the water tank, waitin' for a train." And Mrs. Johnson said, "You know, I used to hear that song when I was a little girl, over at my daddy's grocery store. They'd play that Jimmie Rodgers tune, 'All Around the Water Tank.'" And she said, "I have heard that song *so* many times." And it was a real thrill to me that, right off the bat, some music was played that Mrs. Johnson could relate to. We stayed there for maybe an hour, hour and a half.

JW: *Did you hear Mance Lipscomb on that program?*

DR: Oh yes.

JW: *He was in his seventies.*

DR: Oh yeah, he was a great one. And I know the Secret Service just had fits with President Johnson because he'd go to places like the Kerrville Folk Festival or he'd just wander off and go over and talk to somebody on the street. And for security reasons they didn't want him to do that. "You know," he said, "I can't live in that kind of fear. If they want to get me," he said, "they can get me." He said, "It can happen. I don't think the Secret Service or anybody can totally avoid that. I've got to go ahead and live some kind of a life."

JW: *Yeah.*

DR: He was *deeply* troubled by the war, and marked by it. And I think it kept him from just being a totally happy man. But he'd talk about it at times, and he really thought that if he were ever assassinated, *I* think he thought, it would be somebody who was associated with the Vietnam War.

JW: *He had just had a heart attack earlier that year, as I recall, and this was his first outing.*

DR: He was just coming out of it.

JW: *So this was his first public appearance, wasn't it?*

DR: It was his first public appearance. We only played about four or five holes. He wanted to get out. It was his first time off the ranch after he'd been released from the hospital. He asked if I'd come over and play a few holes of golf. We went to Lady Bird Park, over in Fredericksburg, and played four or five holes—didn't play very much. And then went back to the house, and he took a nap.

We ate dinner, and then went to the show. And the reason he didn't stay longer was he didn't want to push it. It was his first day out, and that was the reason he left early. And I was just hoping that those entertainers would know that, and know the reason. It was phenomenal that he would go to that folk festival anyway. But it was totally understandable why he had to leave.

JW: *Well, he was there for over an hour. The musicians were very impressed, and it was front-page news in the Kerrville paper. Your relationship with President Johnson also brings up another association. This would be an association you might've had. I was thinking about JFK's assassination in Dallas, and that, of course, occurred on the Friday right before the Thanksgiving weekend, which was the big A&M game. What was the impact on you and your football team when those events happened?*

DR: Oh, I remember it clearly. We'd had an early practice, and I'd gone home from the practice field to dress and put on a suit. I was to meet President Kennedy. I was to be the first one to greet him when he stepped off of Air Force One, and I was to present him with an autographed football. [On November 22, 1963, President Kennedy had been scheduled to come to Austin to appear at a

Governor John Connally celebrating UT's national championship with Royal in December 1963, just weeks after Connally, his arm still in a sling, was shot by Lee Harvey Oswald during the assassination of President John Kennedy. Photograph by Bill Malone. Darrell K Royal Papers, CAH, DI01528.

banquet after having visited Dallas.] I was home: I'd showered, and was putting on my tie when it came over the television that the president had been shot. I sat down on the edge of the bed and listened as they were giving the report. And I remember I moved into the living room and sat down in the chair that I watched television from, and stayed there until the conclusion. Then they came back and, of course, said, "The president is dead." And then, talk about what impact it had: there was a lot of talk about canceling the Texas–Texas A&M football game. They came real close to canceling it.

JW: *How did you feel about it?*

DR: I didn't have a feeling. If they wanted to play, we were ready to play. If they wanted to cancel it, I had no objections. That's the kind of call that I didn't feel should come from me or that I should have any input on. That should come from the presidents, the boards of regents, and the chancellors of the two institutions. That's a high-level decision, to make something of that kind.

And, of course, if you remember, we went over there and had a big come-from-behind victory—incidentally, throwing the football. Tommy Wade was our quarterback. He passed us down, and we scored right at the end of the ball game. And in the locker room I got a call from Governor Connally. He was very weak. [One of the bullets fired at Kennedy had hit Connally in the back.] But he had watched part of the ball game, and he knew that we had won. Governor Connally gave me a call in the locker room, and I was able to report that to the squad. They were really thrilled to hear from the governor, as was I, and to hear that he was doing OK and that he felt at least like calling and watching part of the game.

JW: *Well, that's amazing, considering this is on Thursday, November 28.*

DR: Right. Right.

JW: *That's amazing. Well, he was a strong supporter as well and a University of Texas Ex.*

DR: Yes, he was. And he was a good friend. I remember Governor Connally calling me once. We had had a bad year, one of those six-and-four years. We weren't feeling very good, kind of downcast. And he gave me a call and said, "Nellie and I are going over to Lake McQueeney. We are going to go over there and spend a weekend. I would like for you and Edith to go with us. We can just go over and visit, talk, have a good time." So we rode in the car over there with 'em and spent the weekend.

But, Governor Connally never bothered to call me when we were really winning. When we had the bad season, he called me and said, "Let's go for the weekend." That always impressed me about him. He was a good friend, and it was a sad day when we lost him. I went to the funeral, and it was awesome, the people that were there.

JW: *Including President Nixon?*

DR: Right. He sat right in front of me. I didn't get a chance to speak to him. He was two rows in front of me. It wasn't the time to be talking about his trophy. It just wasn't the right time.

Willie

JW: *What about your relationship with—what did President Johnson call them?—"your pickers"? I guess one of the best known of your friends and associates would be musician Willie Nelson. When did you first meet Nelson?*

DR: I heard Willie first when he'd come on package shows to Municipal Auditorium. I used to go to those shows. And he'd be sixth, or something like that, in line on the bill, and he'd only do two or three songs. And I heard him, and knew he was different. The producer of those programs had me backstage, and I met Willie one time, and we visited. I talked to him for a few minutes.

And then I didn't see him again until I heard that he was playing at the Broken Spoke [a well-known country-music dance hall] in Austin. And I decided, well, I'll just go out and see Willie. And that's the first time that I'd ever seen Willie with his band, live, doing a show. I was just totally startled when he started to play. The people quit dancing, and they all walked up to the bandstand and stood in front of him. This was a long time ago. You know, this was *long* before he recorded "Blue Eyes Crying in the Rain."

JW: *Is this still before '72? In the 1960s?*

DR: Oh yeah. And I said, "Gee whiz, this guy's magic! He's really got a following." And I was shocked, because I'd seen him on this package show. So, at the break he'd heard I was there, and he came over to the table and sat down with me. We visited and talked, and he said, "Are you doing anything after we're through here?" And I said, "No, I don't have anything planned." He asked, "Do you want to have a beer?" I said, "Yeah. Yeah, I'd enjoy that." So we went to the club right across the street from the television station where they do *Austin City Limits*. There's a place there that used to be called the Forty Acres Club [now the site of Walter Prescott Webb Hall]. They had a bar in there.

I guess that was about 1972. And I talked to Willie that night. I said, "If we

A jam session at the Royal house in 1991, featuring, from left, Mickey Newbury, Larry Gatlin, Willie Nelson, and Steve Gatlin. Royal, standing behind Newbury, enjoys the music. Photograph by Rick Henson. Darrell K Royal Papers, CAH, DI01537.

Darrell and Willie at their golf tournament, 1991. Photograph by Rick Henson.
Darrell K Royal Papers, CAH, DI01493.

Willie performing in 1978. Photograph by Wally McNamee.
Wally McNamee Photograph Collection, CAH, DI00506.

win the Cotton Bowl, would you come to the game?" He said, "Yeah, I'll come." So, we got in the Cotton Bowl. I gave him a call. He had no idea that we'd won the conference, and hardly remembered telling me he'd come back for the Cotton Bowl, but he did.

JW: *Did he perform at the game?*

DR: No, no. No, he just came back for the game. So we've been partners ever since. He met Joe Jamail then, and he and Joe Jamail and I have been pretty good buddies ever since then. I remember, just before Joe was starting the trial in the Pennzoil-Texaco suit in Houston [in 1985], Willie was in town—he was big by then—and he said, "Let's go see Joe." I said, "I think that'd be great." So we whizzed down to Houston to go see Joe. He stayed up quite late before we left, maybe twelve o'clock. He followed us all the way out to the car and stood out there and talked a long time, and that was just before the big decision. But it was a nice break for him.

A lot of folks have questioned, since I first started running with him, why I would run with Willie Nelson. You know, they seemed to think, I guess, that a football coach at Texas is not supposed to do that, and I always gave 'em the answer. I said, "One of the reasons I like Willie is he forgives me of all my faults." And still likes me. And boy, that just spins their heads big-time. Because, and after all, that's what friends are. You know, I'll betcha you don't have a friend who you like everything he does and everything he says.

JW: *Right.*

DR: But you know, you can have differences of opinions and still get along or, heck, let a guy slide. He makes a mistake—let him slide. And that's what friends do. They let each other make mistakes and still care about you. Sure, there's some things that Willie does that I don't do. Never have and never will.

JW: *And one of the obvious things . . .*

DR: We've discussed it at length.

JW: *Controlled substances, you know. He makes no bones about the fact.*

DR: Yeah. That's right. That's right. And we get along fine.

JW: *And I'm sure that there are people who thought that it was unsavory for you to be associating with him.*

DR: Yeah. Not long ago we were playing chess, and he was smoking. I said, "Do you think that stuff bothers me, just drifting over this way?" He said, "I don't know. Maybe." I said, "Well, I don't feel any different." And we played chess for a little while, and he said, "Coach," he said, "if you ever turned on, would you do it with me? Would you promise me?"

I said, "You got it, Willie. If I ever decide to smoke one of those damned things, I'll do it with you, but don't hold your breath." [laughs]

JW: *[laughs] All right.*

DR: So I never have. I never have even taken a puff of one. I've been in spots where they pass it around, and somebody not knowing tried to pass it to me. I never have even taken it. I just say thank you and no, thank you.

But you know, Willie has so many great qualities. He's generous to a fault with his money. And when he was making big money, he was taking care of a lot of people who needed help. I know one little girl who was in a wheelchair, and she was gonna die if she didn't have this operation. Willie paid for the operation. He didn't even know the kid. She was a big Willie Nelson fan. They had contacted me to get him to sign an album to her. I told him about her circumstances, and he got on the phone and called. He said, "Can you call 'em?" *I* got on the phone and called 'em. And Willie, tears ran down his cheeks when he was talking to those people, and he paid for the operation and had the little girl come up to Billy Bob's [a country-and-western nightclub in Fort Worth] at a concert. She was backstage.

JW: *Great.*

DR: But see, people don't see that side. And I see a kind, generous, caring side of him. You can't write the music he writes and play the music with the feeling that he plays it, and not have deep, strong emotions. I mean, [laughs] it's impossible. A cold person can't write what he writes.

JW: *Now he's had an up-and-down life.*

DR: Oh gosh, has he had an up-and-down life! Yeah. Yeah. "Born in a storm and peace he does despise." [laughs]

JW: *[laughs] That's about the story of his life. You've always been a fan of country music, I guess.*

DR: Yep.

JW: *That's what initially attracted you to Willie?*

DR: Yep, I was talking about the Jimmie Rodgers songs. I heard those same Jimmie Rodgers songs. I remember hearing him on the radio in the '30s when I was, well, about eight, nine, ten years old. I'd hear Jimmie Rodgers, and I've liked it ever since.

JW: *Did you get any criticism? Did anybody suggest that you shouldn't be associated with Willie Nelson?*

DR: Oh yeah, yeah.

JW: *In official circles?*

DR: Yeah. They later came back and, when he got big, wanted to know if I could get him to autograph a picture to their grandkids. I've got an ornery side on something like that. I just said, "I don't know him that well." They were the same ones that criticized me for being with him. Now they want me to get him to autograph a picture. No.

JW: *You did get some flak from the official side here at the university?*

DR: Sure, sure.

JW: *Back around 1990–1991, Willie was deep in the thicket with the IRS over tax problems of about $16 million. I don't want to talk about the specifics of how he got there, but when the IRS came in and seized his property, they put a lot of his property on auction. And one of those properties was the Pedernales Country Club, which you stepped in and bought for about $117,000 at auction. Tell me how all that came about.*

DR: Well, number one, I didn't have $117,000 in cash to go down and buy the thing. I called Jim Bob [Moffett] and told him what the situation was. He said, "I'll get a cashier's check to you." So, he did. I found him in Europe. But he worked it out, and I got a cashier's check, went down, and bought the property at the courthouse steps. But the IRS had the right of redemption, which means that they had 120 days to advertise the property, and if somebody paid more for it than the $117,000, then they could pay me off and accept the higher bid.

JW: *That was a very, very inexpensive price for that country club then.*

DR: It was. Oh yeah. That's what Jim Bob asked: "Is it worth it?" I said, "Yes. It's worth it as an investment if, in fact, we wind up owning the thing." But it helped Willie over a spot. Willie would've done the same thing for me. He'd've done the same thing for Jim Bob. Willie's always been generous and a

Royal and Willie share a private moment at one of their favorite places, the golf course, in the mid-1990s. Darrell K Royal Papers, CAH, DI01481.

good guy to help somebody he likes who really needs help. You know, talking about that IRS thing, I was playing chess with him one time, and he laughed. He said, "You know, I think this is all kind of funny." He said, "You know, I grew up over there picking cotton, trying to learn to play a guitar, from real poor circumstances." He said, "Nobody would've ever dreamed that some day I could owe $17 million." He said, "I think it's kind of funny that a guy from my circumstances could be $17 million in debt." [laughs]

JW: *I'm glad he could laugh. [laughs]*

DR: Well, that's the way he laughed about it. But actually he owed two million, and all the others were penalties and fines. And he really didn't realize that he owed the money. He thought his taxes had been paid.

JW: *He had a financial management company.*

DR: A guy named Neil Reshen, an agent out of New York, was handling his affairs then. The Price Waterhouse thing, what happened when he owed the two million, he had the cash to pay it. And he wanted to go ahead and pay it, but his managers and his advisers said, "Make this investment with Price Waterhouse." I don't know all the ramifications of it. There was a lawsuit over that. But he loses the $15 million in a cattle-feed operation, and now he *can't* pay the taxes. All of his money's gone. He could've paid. Well, the cattle operation was a big loser, and he loses all his money, and now this thing starts, all the back fines and penalties. It was just growing and growing and growing. It grows 20 percent a year or over 20 percent a year. When you get into those figures, it starts growing in a hurry.

JW: *What's the sequel to this story about the country club? What eventually happened?*

DR: There was an Iranian who bought it from the IRS. And apparently he thought he could make Willie do tricks if he owned that country club or owned that little nine-hole golf course and recording studio. But he just didn't know Willie at all. I mean, he's not going to control Willie in any shape, form, or fashion. So what happened? Well, the guy didn't have any equipment to cut the grass or anything else, so all of Willie's people just quit. And they took all their equipment and locked it up, and that thing grew up in pasture real quick. And the studio was dilapidated and gone. The Iranian was asking a big price to sell it. His price came down pretty fast, and he winds up losing money, and somebody bought it cheaper than what he paid for it, but some of Willie's friends bought it. And it's back, cleaned up, in operation, and the studio's been refurbished and new equipment put in.

JW: *Yes. I've been out to see it. And a lot of other projects are going on there at the same time.*

DR: Yeah, that's right. A lot of people are going out there recording, and the golf course is being maintained, and so Willie's right back just like he was.

JW: *Is he pretty much out of the woods now on his tax situation, or getting there?*

DR: Yeah, he's got it worked out. He's got it worked out. But you know, his personality never changed. I never saw him despondent or down. He was able to laugh about it and go on. But material things never have meant much to Willie anyway. You know, how can you tell if he's broke? He dresses the same if he's got millions or if he's broke. [laughs]

JW: *T-shirt and running shoes, yeah.*

DR: Yeah. [laughs] That's the way he is. That's all he wants. He's an unusual guy. He's a study. He's an interesting person. But material things never have meant that much to him. They really don't. He abuses 'em pretty badly [laughs]

JW: *[laughs]*

DR: He's hard on money. [laughs] He gives it to people; he doesn't keep track of it. Willie had an operation on his hand recently [2004], and he's been in Hawaii recuperating. I've talked to him on the phone.

JW: *Well, I understand it was like carpal tunnel syndrome, like a lot of those computer-related repetitive-motion injuries.*

DR: Well, you know, Willie uses his left hand a lot, bending his wrist, chordin', and playing the neck of the guitar. And he plays it so well. He hit a lot of different notes. So it finally got him. But as far as I know, the operation was highly successful, and he's well on his way to recovery.

JW: *It's interesting you talking about turning his left wrist like that to strike those chords on the frets of the guitar. That tells me he's a real guitar player, because I've seen so many people cheat just by using their thumb to lay over.*

DR: No, no, no.

JW: *A real guitarist gets those fingers curled over the frets.*

DR: Oh. Well, I've seen Willie do it many, many times, where he has nearly his whole hand up on top of the neck of the guitar. His wrist is just bowed back around there. He put a lot of strain on his hand.

Tragedies

JW: *You've had a pretty rough life. A couple of your kids died tragically in automobile accidents. And I was thinking, particularly, about 1973. Was that the year that your daughter had that accident?*

DR: My son, David. He was killed on a motorcycle.

JW: *Was that in 1983?*

DR: I don't know the exact year.

JW: *I thought the first tragedy was your daughter with a shuttle bus accident.*

DR: That's right.

JW: *That came in the spring, which must've been a particularly hard time for you because you're supposed to be intensely involved in recruiting. What sort of impact did that have on your decision finally to leave coaching?*

DR: Well, I don't think it had anything to do with me leaving coaching, but it softens your approach. Makes you understand that some things are not as important as you thought they were. Made me look at what I was doing in the game and the intensity and that maybe—maybe—it wasn't all that important. I think I eased back and became a little bit softer and not quite as aggressive after that as a coach. And I don't know. I know that we weren't as demanding probably after that, or I wasn't.

(Editor's note: Daughter Marian Royal Kazen died as the result of an automobile collision in April 1973. Son David W. Royal died as the result of a motorcycle accident in March 1982. Both accidents occurred in Austin.)

"Climbing Is a Thrill. Maintaining Is a Bitch."

JW: *What led you to decide that you wanted to retire from coaching? What were the factors that led up to that?*

DR: Well, it got so that winning wasn't exciting and losing became intolerable. When I first came here at age thirty-two, we'd have a win, and, man, I was so high and so happy and just thrilled beyond words. At the last, when we'd win a ball game it was just, boy, I'm glad that's over—we didn't lose. I didn't have the same thrill. I used to bounce back from a loss. We'd lose a ball game, and I'd be dejected Sunday, and by Monday I was ready to go back and go after the next contest. And at the last it got so that losses just ate at me, and it was just miserable.

And the mix wasn't there. We were getting ready to play Texas Tech up there in their sold-out stadium on national television. I used to just *love* that kind of a contest—I wanted to get in that kind of a contest. But the feeling then was kind of like, boy, I hope we can get over this. You know, and Earl was hurt.

JW: *That was Earl Campbell?*

DR: Yeah, he had pulled hamstrings and hadn't played until then, and he was ready to go. Sold-out stadium, national television. I ought to have been excited. I ought to have been looking forward to going to that contest, really wanting to go to it. And I thought the mix just wasn't the same, and I just thought it was time. I thought about it a long time. I didn't rush into it—it wasn't a quick decision. I'd been thinking about it for a year.

JW: *You finally retired when?*

DR: After the 1976 season.

JW: *There's one very poignant image that's often reported about the latter period. It may have been the Oklahoma game, up in Dallas at the Cotton Bowl. And they reported that after the game was over, it was that tie game.*

Royal and his players after his last game as coach, 1976. UT defeated Arkansas 29–12. Photograph by Ron Meredeith. Darrell K Royal Papers, CAH, DI01561.

Two college football coaching legends, Frank Broyles of Arkansas and Darrell Royal of UT, before their game in December 1976 at Memorial Stadium in Austin. After the game, each announced his retirement from coaching. The two coaches met twenty times, with Royal's Longhorns winning fifteen of those games. Royal departed as the winningest coach in the history of the now-defunct Southwest Conference. DI01489. Darrell K Royal Papers, CAH, DI01489.

DR: Six to six.

JW: *Six-six tie. They said that you were seen with the dry heaves on the sideline, totally exhausted and spent by the experience. Do you recall that happening?*

DR: Yeah, there were a number of things going on. But it wasn't the same. Basically, it wasn't as big a thrill to win as it used to be. Losses were a lot harder to take. It's harder to maintain than it is to climb. Climbing is a thrill. Maintaining is a bitch.

JW: *That was ultimately what led to your decision?*

DR: Yeah, that was it. A lot of factors, a lot of different things, a lot of different reasons—there are a lot of things involved that I could get into, but that sums it up.

JW: *Did you get any pressure from the university to consider retiring, before you made your decision?*

DR: No, never. Hell, we'd just been to the Cotton Bowl seven out of the last nine years. [laughs] What kind of pressure was I under? One bad year, which we had our last year. That doesn't put you under heat. No, the only pressure I got was to *not* do it.

JW: *When you did decide to retire, you did it at the same time as Frank Broyles.*

DR: Yes. I have a rapport with Frank Broyles, whom I competed against nineteen times. Frank Broyles and I never had an argument. We never had a disagreement, and we're still good friends today and still vacation together. That's when football is fun, when you have that kind of rapport with the people whom you're competing against.

Bear Bryant

JW: *One of your old nemeses, back here in the earlier days, was Bear Bryant, who was at Texas A&M first, then later went on to Alabama, where, I must say, he was elevated to the status of a local saint. [laughs]*

DR: Yep.

JW: *What sort of relationship did you have with Bear Bryant, on the field and off?*

DR: Well, I first met him just after I graduated from the University of Oklahoma. Spring practice was taking place, and he was coaching at Kentucky. And obviously I wasn't involved in spring practice, but I showed up to a couple of the practices, and there was Coach Bryant. Coach Wilkinson asked me to just stay with Coach Bryant, walk around with him at practice, and answer any questions about what we were doing as I saw it as a player—why we did this drill and what we were trying to accomplish. And so I did that. He was there for three or four days. So I got to know him real well over that three or four days, as a guy just graduating from college and interested in going into coaching. And it was a great association because he was an established coach and well known, and he had a chance to really help me advance in the coaching profession by talking about me, saying nice things about me, being complimentary, and that type of thing.

Then later I came to the University of Texas, and he was the only person I heard from, from the other schools, welcoming me into the conference. I got a wire from him. He said, "Welcome to the Southwest Conference family. Glad to have you aboard." Of course, we played them his last year before he went to Alabama. Our Texas team played over at College Station. We competed a number of times in bowl games after that.

JW: *And as I recall, you bested him in 1964.*

DR: Well, 1957 was our first encounter, over at College Station. They had John David Crow and Charlie Krueger and that crowd.

JW: *John David Crow later won a Heisman Trophy.*

DR: Heisman Trophy winner, yeah. Then I guess the next time was in the Orange Bowl, and then the next time was in the Bluebonnet Bowl, and the next time was in the Cotton Bowl.

JW: *So did you manage to beat him a few times?*

DR: We tied one and we won three.

JW: *Good record.*

DR: Yes.

JW: *Have you seen the museum they have for him there at Alabama?*

Longhorn players carry Royal off the field after their 17–13 victory over Alabama in the 1973 Cotton Bowl. The Crimson Tide, ranked fourth, couldn't overcome the seventh-ranked Longhorns' strong running attack, led by quarterback Alan Lowry and running back Roosevelt Leeks. It was the last of four meetings between Royal and Bear Bryant. Royal never lost. Prints and Photographs Collection, CAH, CT0123.

Royal and Alabama coach Paul "Bear" Bryant after the fifth-ranked Longhorns defeated top-ranked Alabama 21–17 in the Orange Bowl in Miami, Florida, January 1, 1965. Alabama, led by All-American quarterback Joe Namath, fell behind quickly 21–7 and couldn't recover as the Longhorns held on for the win. Photograph by Flip Schulke, © Sports Illustrated *magazine. Darrell K Royal Papers, CAH, CN09410.*

DR: I haven't seen it. But he was the kind of guy who had that type of personality, and he sure got a lot of attention. And he had a tremendous record.

JW: *Yes.*

DR: Talking about the wishbone formation earlier, I think it lengthened his coaching career by maybe ten years. He got the wishbone from us here, and he had *phenomenal* success with it. He won a number of national championships with the wishbone.

JW: *He's one of those coaches—there are several you could probably name— who coached well into their later years.*

DR: Yeah, he was 70. And of course he died less than a year after he resigned. That was another thing: I didn't want to coach that long. I wanted to do other things. I wanted to have some free time while I was healthy and to do what I wanted to do. That had a lot to do with my decision.

Retirement

JW: *When you resigned as the head coach, you were still athletic director.*

DR: Yes.

JW: *And you remained athletic director for a couple more years?*

DR: Two more years.

JW: *What ultimately led you to leave the athletic directorship?*

DR: I started thinking about that, right after I got into just the athletic directorship. I knew that I wasn't cut out to be just an athletic director. I didn't like the paperwork; I didn't like the meetings; I didn't like the rule books; I didn't like the NCAA meetings, Southwest Conference meetings, all the meetings, at the university level. I didn't like sitting behind a desk; I didn't like writing letters; I didn't like talking on the telephone.

I'd been used to being in the eye of the storm, and I quickly saw that I wasn't cut out to be just an athletic director. I'd thought that maybe some day I would retire and just stay as athletic director, and then finish out doing that. But I tried it for a couple of years, and then resigned from that.

JW: *One of the issues that came up during your tenure as the athletic director was the role of other sports, besides the football program, competing for funds and resources on the university campus. Did you have to deal with those issues of allocations of resources to other programs? For example, women's athletics and other sports?*

DR: I think I had a big influence on that, that we were not combined. Women's athletics programs had a total separate department, and I had nothing to do with that, and that's the way I wanted it. I didn't want 'em to be combined. They had their own athletic council, their own athletic director, and

Fifty-two-year old Coach Royal during his last game as coach, against Arkansas in 1976. Photograph by Ron Meredeith. Darrell K Royal Papers, CAH, DI01562.

their own budget, and that was run by the university administration. We made contributions to their cause, but had nothing to say about how it was spent, didn't want to have anything to say how it was spent. So women's athletics was totally separate.

As far as other sports are concerned, we gave what money we could, what money we made. I'm happy to say we made a little money or broke even every year because we had winning football programs, and we were able to support the other non-revenue-bearing sports. But I had something to do with the hiring of people who were the coaches of those sports. But once they were hired, my role as athletic director was to just tell 'em what their budget was, tell 'em to abide by the rules, and then get the hell out of their way and leave 'em alone. And I never bothered with the other coaches. I think if you go ask 'em what kind of athletic director I was, I wasn't in their way. I was busy coaching football. I never had a moment's conflict with Cliff Gustafson, for instance. As athletic director, I hired him as our baseball coach. Cliff ran a clean program. Cliff stayed within his budget. Cliff won baseball games. It was none of my business when they worked out. That was between him and his players. It was the same with Abe Lemons, the basketball coach.

JW: *What were the circumstances leading to Lemons's departure?*

DR: I wasn't here then. I wasn't the athletic director.

JW: *That's right. He was another very colorful figure.*

DR: Yeah. Oh yeah.

JW: *Quotable quotes, if ever.*

DR: And I think I made the right hire. He packed 'em in that arena.

JW: *And went to the NIT.*

DR: And won it.

JW: *That was a rare thing for Longhorn basketball, at that time.*

DR: Yeah, it was.

JW: *It took a long time to get back to the NCAA.*

DR: We went from a losing sport to a revenue-bearing sport, quickly. But I never asked Abe how much of a problem I gave him. I just didn't. I mean, he was his own coach. I didn't expect anybody to be bothering me when I was coaching football—had I not *been* athletic director—as long as I was doing two things: staying within the budget and within the rules.

JW: *What, then, were the factors that led to your decision to retire as athletic director?*

DR: I just didn't *like* being athletic director. I didn't like it.

JW: *Did you receive any pressure to resign?*

DR: Nope.

JW: *It was entirely your decision?*

DR: My decision, 100 percent.

JW: *When you did retire, you ultimately became a special assistant to the university president. How did that come about? What does the job involve?*

DR: Well, it's varied, and hard to explain. I'm on call from the president. I'm special assistant to the president on athletic affairs: if they want to talk about past history or how we got into these types of contracts of who we were playing—or if they want me to go to any kind of function.

I visit with DeLoss Dodds [the current athletic director] all the time. But he calls me; I never go in and tell him what I think. He has to ask me. And neither do I have the gall to tell the university president what I think. They call *me* and ask. And I go to a number of alumni functions.

A few years ago, I wrote a letter that was scattered all over the state. We put a PAC together to help people in the legislature who were interested in higher education. It's a shame we had to do that. But they told me it was important that we do it. I wrote that letter, and we had a great response, an unbelievable response from people who sent money in for that cause. I sit on a board of trustees. The University of Texas received a lot of money from that board. I sit on another board of trustees that awards scholarships to Texas and Texas A&M. We award twenty or so scholarships every year to the University of Texas. These scholarships average between $6,000 and $7,000 a year, so they're good scholarships.

Well, I feel like that's university time. When I'm spending time on that and getting students here, on that deal, I know I've been called on. I'm not a fundraiser. But I've been called on to contact certain individuals about their giving to the university, and I've been successful doing that.

Houston lawyer Joe Jamail and Darrell Royal, 1996.
Darrell K Royal Papers, CAH, DI01494.

JW: *So there is a large fund-raising element to that.*

DR: I don't have set office hours, but my position is productive. They've more than paid for my part-time salary. But I would do that anyway, even if I didn't have the position. I would do it just because I enjoy doing it for the university.

JW: *Who was the president at the time this special-assistant position was set up?*

DR: Peter Flawn.

JW: *Was this at his suggestion? Whose idea was this?*

DR: Yeah, his. I stayed on half-time. See, I was on full-time as special assistant, and I did more then. But I retired. I took full retirement, and now I'm on a part-time basis. My salary is not any big number, [laughs] you know.

JW: *When you visit the Longhorn football team practices, what do you say to the coaches?*

DR: I don't say anything. The coaches are nice enough to explain to me what they're doing and what they're trying to accomplish. I see a lot of time-saving drills that have been instituted since my coaching days. And I just wondered, why didn't we think of having the drill in this manner so we could get in more repetitions? That's what practice is for, to repeat over and over situations that you're going to see in an actual game. And the more repetitions you get, the better off the drill. I never liked coaches to stop and coach players after every move they made. It takes time away from them repeating it over and over and over till it gets so they don't have to think in those situations: they just react, and react to something that they learned in a drill.

JW: *This is something you've seen in the drills.*

DR: I've seen some drills since Coach Brown's been here. I've seen some excellent drills that are time-savers, and they're good teaching methods, things that I would do if I had it to do over again.

JW: *Of course, back in your day you didn't have a big all-weather dome to work in. [laughs]*

DR: No. That covered practice field lets you practice regardless of the weather. That's the nice thing about it. Before we had the dome, if it came a hard rain, you missed a practice. We used to go to Gregory Gym or somewhere like that, some place you could find that you could work inside a little bit. Put sneakers on them and kind of run through the drills. But now they've got the Astroturf in that dome, and if it rains they can still have a real good practice session.

JW: *What sort of relationship do you have with the current UT administration, as a special assistant to the president for athletic programs?*

DR: Very good. I like Larry Faulkner, the president, a lot. I have pinch-hit for him in some situations where he couldn't go to an ex-students' meeting. I do that type of thing. Dr. Faulkner and I get along real well.

JW: *Has your role grown in any way over the years as you've been involved in this?*

DR: No, no, no. On the contrary, I've been involved a little bit less and a little bit less. But you know, I have such an interest in the Longhorns and all sports that it'll never totally go away.

JW: *I think you may be underestimating your role in showing up to UT football practices, for example. I think your just being there is an inspiration to the kids in a very intangible way. You don't have to say or instruct them so much as just be there and give them a few words of encouragement.*

DR: Well, I don't think much about it from that angle. I go because I enjoy the practice sessions and enjoy watching 'em work and watching the drills that they go through. And it's fun. I go maybe once a week, if that. But when they're practicing, I enjoy going occasionally to watch the coaches work.

JW: *When they play home football games, do you watch from the stands, from home, or on the sidelines? Where are you?*

DR: I'm usually in Joe Jamail's box, and I kind of move around. I kind of suite-hop when I'm up there. At halftime or before the game, I go say hello to different people, and I just have a good visit. When the game's actually going on, I like to sit down. I don't like to talk much. I like to watch the game.

Politics

JW: *Earlier you were talking about the need as a University of Texas football coach to be aware not only of athletics, but also of the political climate surrounding you, and you said that D. X. Bible took you aside when you first showed up. What did he say to you?*

DR: He said, "Darrell, stay away from the Capitol." He said, "Those are good people, but to be involved in politics is not good for a football coach at the University of Texas," and that's what he meant. He didn't mean don't be with 'em socially, meet 'em socially, and, of course, vote, and all those things. He definitely believed in being a good citizen and a good community citizen, and you've got to know something about politics to do that. He didn't say don't be politically aware. He just said stay away from the Capitol. Of course, he had no idea how political it was going to become in Austin years later. [laughs]

But I think what he meant was to not endorse political candidates publicly. That can be a divisive thing because, as a guy coaching at the University of Texas, I now understand, you need the support of Democrats and Republicans. All facets come through in support of the University of Texas, and to align yourself with a particular group kind of turns a cold shoulder to another just-as-important group to you. And I think that's what he was talking about.

JW: *And in a sense, you're almost like a public figure in the political world, in that you really do have a constituency, a broad one that you have to serve, and you cannot be seen to be playing favorites.*

DR: You know, I don't know if I've mentioned this before, but I did a commercial for an automobile. It was Chrysler, and I didn't think anything about it. But I soon found out that we had a lot of Texas boosters who sold Fords and Chevrolets and the other cars, and it wasn't wise for me to be endorsing a product. And I got away from *that* quickly.

The Southwest Conference and the Business of College Athletics

JW: *The Southwest Conference is history now. Of course, first Arkansas withdrew from the Southwest Conference and went to the Southeastern Conference. And as far back as 1990 you pretty much predicted all of that was going to happen. Why don't you tell me about what happened to the Southwest Conference, which, during your coaching tenure, was so strong. Certainly your teams came in with three national championships and got their share of the limelight, and the competition seemed to be pretty good. What happened to the Southwest Conference over the years that led to this?*

DR: Well, the conference broke up when Arkansas left. That was the old Southwest Conference, and when they left, a big chunk of it left, and then the pieces started to come apart. But I don't know why it happened. Some of the schools simply couldn't draw crowds. I know when I first came here, our three big ball games were with Oklahoma, Texas A&M, and Rice. Arkansas wasn't that big a ball game. The Texas-Arkansas game became big after Frank Broyles came to Arkansas and started being really competitive.

The Rice game was always sold out. I remember distinctly being down on the field in warm-ups talking to Coach Jess Neely. He said, "I don't know if the fire marshal's gonna shut us down tonight or not, because I told 'em to go ahead and sell seats in the aisle." They literally had sold all the seats in the stadium, and people still wanted to come. So he sold 'em admission to go sit in the aisles, and they understood that they'd have to sit in the aisles. I looked up, and sure in heck there they were, sitting in the aisles. Now, that game deteriorated to where it didn't draw.

More importantly, the competition between, say, Rice and TCU had no attendance at all. SMU-TCU had no attendance, nor did TCU-Houston. Those crowds that dwindle down to almost high school crowds are used by outside recruiters, and they come and say, "Well, gosh. You want to play in that kind of

Three coaching legends: Royal, Bud Wilkinson, and Frank Broyles, December 1970. Prints and Photographs Collection, CAH, CN07536.

environment? Let me show you the attendance at these schools. Who's going to see you play?" So they took talent away from this state.

Again, back when the Southwest Conference was strong and when it was good, Oklahoma would get a few, Arkansas would get a few, and Notre Dame would get a few. Now, everybody in the nation's drawing from Texas. One year I saw where five went to Stanford, five went to Tennessee, four went to Florida State. They go to Nebraska, they go to Colorado. The talent was just leaving the state in droves. And, we couldn't be a strong conference unless we kept those people at home. It was past the point of keeping 'em home, because of the attendance thing and the lack of television exposure, and it was going to get so that the University of Texas was not gonna be able to be on television if they stayed in that conference. Texas A&M wouldn't be able to be on television unless we were playing each other, and it's a money game.

And people say, "Well, I hate to see intercollegiate athletics come down to just money issues." Well, it's always been money. Now, you don't spend appropriated money. You've got to earn your own way. And then on top of that comes the gender-equity thing; a lot of that burden's being placed on men's athletics programs, to support women's athletics. It was mandatory that Texas and Texas A&M move to a situation where they could get a good TV package and get that income to take care of these added expenses. Now, had we moved sooner, we would've had to move just as a pair, I think. But by delaying it, we were able to take some of the Southwest Conference members with us. We were able to take Baylor and Texas Tech. I think if we'd have left at the same time Arkansas did, we wouldn't have been able to take those two schools, and I'm glad that at least we were able to keep four of us together.

People ask me am I saddened. Sure, I'm saddened. I think about guys like Jess Neely, who I mentioned before, and Abe Martin at TCU and the good relationships we had with them. Matty Bell was athletic director up at SMU when the conference was strong. It wasn't unusual for us to have as many as three, sometimes four, teams in the top ten in the nation. It was just a few years back, when we played Arkansas in 1969, that we were ranked one-two.

JW: *That's right.*

DR: But that's disappeared. It's gone. And the only decision that Texas and Texas A&M and Baylor and Texas Tech had was to align with a conference where you could get a big-money TV package, if they were gonna stay alive and stay competitive in big-time athletics.

JW: *Let's put a little more perspective on the TV coverage. What in financial terms does national television exposure mean to a team like the University of Texas?*

DR: Well, it's advertising. When you're on there, people know about you, and those players understand that. These high school recruits, they want to go where they're exposed, where they can make a name for themselves, and that's the reason they were leaving the state in droves.

JW: *How did the television coverage change over the years? Did you used to have sort of unlimited access to television coverage?*

DR: No, it's always been controlled by the NCAA. There was a group that broke off and was called the College Football Association, the CFA, and the CFA had a television package. Well, that was a smaller group than, say, the total NCAA. Well, now the CFA has been spread around by too many different schools. And what's happened now with this alliance of these conferences, it's boiling down to instead of having about sixty or sixty-five schools in the CFA, it's now down to maybe forty or fifty schools.

JW: *You would see those teams over and over again, and there would be no variety.*

DR: You'll see those teams over and over again, and you won't be sharing the money with the other people. It becomes the haves and have-nots, actually.

JW: *This was sort of an elite core of teams.*

DR: That's right. That's exactly the reason they call it a superconference. The biggies get together and form their own league and then get their own TV package.

JW: *Let's talk about how this new alignment works logistically. Here's Texas and A&M and Baylor and Tech in the Big Eight Conference, which, as a conference, had traditional rivals: Oklahoma, Colorado, Missouri, and other teams like that. Why did Texas go to this conference rather than the Pacific-10 Conference?*

DR: The average distance to the Big Eight schools, if you figure it out from Austin, Texas, is 590 miles. If we'd've gone to the Pac-10, the *closest* school to us is 1,250 miles, and then you start traveling from there. Then you've got to go on. After you get into Arizona, then you've got a long ways to Seattle and Oregon and the schools that are located up in there. So, distance-wise, we haven't expanded that much.

Going to Norman and Stillwater is not that much different from going to Lubbock. And you have the Texas-Oklahoma game. We think about that immediately. Then where's that going to be played? Well, it doesn't make sense to move the game. It's too profitable. Texas and Oklahoma each make a large amount of extra money by playing that game in Dallas. They're not going to put that on a home-and-home basis. The Texas and Oklahoma game was too big to lose. And the Texas–Texas A&M game was too big to lose. They had to keep some of those games intact. It took a long time sitting at the table, but they worked it out.

JW: *This really combines two things here: the element of tradition as well as financial and practical considerations.*

DR: Yes, it does.

JW: *I want to go back and look at one of the things that's led to this situation: recruiting. Now you said back during your coaching days, in the 1970s, that only a few outside schools such as Notre Dame were recruiting Texas talent, so there really wasn't a big outflow of talent. Is there anything that you can point to that changed this? And how did these other schools started recruiting so heavily in Texas?*

DR: They came in and they said, "Look. Here are the schools you're playing against: SMU." And they gave their attendance. Their capacity's only about 20,000.

JW: *At that little stadium. [From 1989 to 1994, SMU played its home football games at Ownby Stadium, which held around 20,000.]*

DR: At that little stadium. And Houston doesn't draw. Rice doesn't draw. TCU doesn't draw. They show those meager crowds, and they say, "This is the conference you want to play in?" You know. "How many times have you seen these people on television? But contrasted to that, look at our attendance of all of our schools, and see how many times we're on television. You're going to be getting a lot of exposure if you come to our place."

JW: *When did Rice, for example, start losing attendance? They were doing well a number of years ago.*

DR: Well, they were doing well when they could win, you know. And when you play a contest like the Texas-Rice game and you go twenty-five years without a victory, people lose interest in it. We used to get our head whopped around pretty good when Jess Neely was at Rice. They didn't win every year or every other year, but they'd win about one out of three or one out of four.

JW: *Well, they were recruiting talent at that time.*

DR: They were recruiting talent. They definitely were.

JW: *And I guess what I'm trying to get at is a school like Rice didn't have talent to work with as much as before.*

DR: I can't tell you that. I can't give you the answer for that. I really don't know. I've thought about it and thought about it. I didn't experience the Rice situation, so I don't know.

JW: *But it was happening in several schools. Obviously in the case of SMU, they went through that death-penalty experience. [In 1986 the NCAA punished the SMU football program with "death penalty" sanctions for repeated, flagrant rule violations. In the first year of the punishment, all football games were canceled; during the second year, the team could play only away games. SMU chose to cancel all games the second year, also.]*

DR: It *was* a death penalty.

JW: *It pretty well devastated their program.*

DR: It was accurately named. It was a death penalty.

JW: *The fact that it was applied in the case of SMU on such a high-profile basis, do you think that resonated throughout the coaching community nationwide?*

DR: I think they've decided not to do it again, be my guess. I haven't seen anybody else threatened with the death penalty. I think they've realized that's so severe. I doubt if they'll ever get back up to where they were.

JW: *So, I'm now seeing the meaning behind your words. I saw you interviewed on the local news the day that they announced that the conference would be dividing, and you came out with one of your great quotable quotes. You said, "Humpty Dumpty's broke. You've gotta move on."*

DR: Yeah, we can't put him back together again. That's it. You just can't do it. I mean, we tried and tried, and we hung in there as long as we could. All the leaves were getting brown on the edges and getting ready to wither and die; if we didn't make a move, we were gonna wither and die with 'em. I'm talking about Texas and Texas A&M and Baylor and Texas Tech.

JW: *You have been a special assistant to the university president here for some years, and, of course, they call on you for advice on various things. Did you have any role at all in the decision ultimately about what to do?*

DR: Nothing, other than just visiting and talking when we'd see each other. But as far as being called in and having a vote, no. I would see DeLoss Dodds, and we'd talk about it. I'd see Bill Cunningham, who was the chancellor then, and we'd talk about it. I'd see Robert Berdahl, who was the president, and we'd talk about it. But I was for moving. I was for doing something—I was for doing something several years ago. But I think now, in hindsight, I think we were wise to hold on because we were able to take Texas Tech and Baylor, and we would've had to leave them behind before.

This was a big change for football, but basketball was affected even more. When you throw Texas in with Kansas and Missouri and Kansas State and Oklahoma and Oklahoma State, you're talking about some powerful basketball.

JW: *Do you think that the basketball competition in the Southwest Conference also suffered from that image nationwide of being subpar?*

DR: Yes. Yes, I do. Our basketball coach at the time, Tom Penders, had to guard what he said, but he was pretty vocal about the Southwest Conference. I think he was delighted to have us join the new conference and to get in a little bit swifter current.

JW: *Obviously the recruiting has been the same in basketball. You see Texas players on squads all over the nation. In Michigan, for example.*

DR: Sure. Right here, taking 'em right out of Austin. And taking football players out of Austin to Florida State. You know, that was unheard of twenty years ago, but now it's commonplace.

JW: *How do you think things are going in the Big Twelve since Texas joined the conference?*

DR: Well, let me say first of all that I'm not well informed with the workings of the Big Twelve. Obviously I'm not involved in any of their meetings, and I see the Big Twelve as any other fan would see it. It's been a great concept, and I think it's worked out tremendously well. If you check the ratings of the conferences, the Big Twelve rates as one of the better conferences, if not the best, in the United States.

JW: *So I guess it was a natural move, even though a lot of people lament the loss of the Southwest Conference. But it does seem to have worked out okay.*

DR: Well, I notice the crowds are still there. [laughs] They're selling plenty of tickets.

JW: *Coach, how much are you involved in the Longhorn football program these days?*

DR: Well, I don't work on a daily basis anymore, so I'm not informed. I don't know all the intricacies that take place *in* the conference, and to tell you frankly, at my age, I wouldn't want to be involved.

JW: *Just for the record, how old are you now?*

DR: Well, if I make it till July 6 [2004], I'll be 80.

JW: *I think you'll make it. [Royal laughs.] You're looking pretty good.*

DR: [laughs] I think I'll make it.

JW: *You mentioned the financial situation while talking about the Southwest Conference. One aspect of that is gender equity, which is associated with Title IX, in women's athletics. We talked earlier about this during your tenure as athletic director, and some of these issues were just beginning to come up in the '70s. What was the contribution or the role of the movement for gender equity in college athletics? How did that contribute to the new situation, the way you saw it?*

DR: Well, it's a *tremendous* financial burden. I know I was called to the White House when President Ford was in office and Title IX was passed. And Bo Schembechler and maybe two more of us went to the White House and met with President Ford. And I knew my only thought and comment at the time was that I doubted that the lawmakers really understood what kind of a law they had passed, because the cost was going to be large, and I didn't know who was going to pay for this cost. Men's athletics was paying for itself, by gate receipt and ticket sales. Was the university going to take over that burden for financing women's athletics? It's the law. It's going to have to be complied with.

The question is who's going to supply the money. If men's athletics is required to fund women's athletics, then we're going to wind up playing just those sports that produce revenue for the men and eliminating all those sports that are non-revenue-bearing, that cost money. You're going to have to eliminate everything except football, basketball, and, possibly, baseball. I think baseball about breaks even. But for every scholarship you have in baseball, then you have to have a scholarship for the women. So that would make it so that there wasn't enough money. It didn't make enough money to support the scholarship for baseball and then a scholarship for women. It didn't make *that* much money, I know. It didn't make enough money to support two scholarships instead of one.

I was afraid you might have to drop baseball, and we would wind up just playing football and basketball. And then the women will have track and tennis and swimming, the sports that men can't have. Like I said, I don't think they knew at the time what kind of a law they had passed.

JW: *Right.*

DR: And I'm not opposed to women's athletics. I'm just as much in favor of them competing, and I think they derive every benefit that men do. The only question in my mind was who's going to pay for it.

JW: *I think this was a big question before, say, women's basketball had established itself. I think it is fairly well established now. And here at the University of Texas, for example, do you feel that the situation has improved because the women's basketball team can fill the Erwin Center for a given game?*

DR: Fill it?

JW: *Well, not fill it, but turn in the crowd.*

DR: Well, you said fill it.

JW: *Yeah.*

DR: [laughs] There's a difference in filling it and making expenses. You know?

JW: *There was a while there that they were outdrawing the men's team, when the men's team was at sort of a low point.*

DR: How much money were they making?

JW: *I don't know.*

DR: It comes back to money. They weren't covering all their expenses.

JW: *And so just a single sport, like basketball, being fairly successful is not enough to really cover the whole athletic program?*

DR: Oh no. Heavens no. I don't know what their total income would be for all sports. It sounds like I'm rapping women's athletics. I'm really not. It's just a question of who's going to pay for it. I think it's fine. But if they're going to drain men's athletics by expecting them to pay for it, then they're going to have to quit playing anything except football and basketball.

JW: *This law that Title IX is part of was passed during the Ford administration in the mid-1970s.*

DR: Yes, yes.

JW: *So you were still athletic director?*

DR: I was still the athletic director, and that was the reason I was called up there.

JW: *Right. But you were still coach, as a matter of fact.*

DR: Yeah. I was coaching and athletic director.

JW: *Let's talk about the Bowl Championship Series, which is known as the BCS. This past year [2003] brought up a lot of the issues again about a national college football championship because there was some dispute about who was really number one. Oklahoma suffered a loss right before their Sugar Bowl game, and the Rose Bowl had a national contender in it. In other words, this issue came up again about who's really the national champion. And of course they always say, "We ought to have a playoff." What do you think about it?*

DR: You know, they used to just vote on it. They had the AP poll, the UPI poll, and the coaches' poll. I think that worked as well as any playoff system they've devised. Ever since they've had a playoff system, there's been a hitch in it, there've been complaints about it, and I never heard so much talk as I have about the BCS in 2003. In any type of system where you vote people *in* to the playoff, somebody's gonna be left out, somebody's gonna be unhappy. Let me say, I don't have an answer. I just know there hasn't been a real good answer yet.

JW: *Were you satisfied with the old system, just a poll of sportswriters and coaches?*

DR: There were fewer complaints about it.

JW: *[laughs] I suppose you're right.*

DR: So it apparently worked better.

JW: *I know that during your coaching tenure you were very concerned about the academic side as well of student athletes. Would you be worried about adding additional games if they tried to do a playoff?*

DR: Yeah, I think it would be wrong to have a playoff system taking place during final examinations. You know, we used to have the bowl system. We had our regular season—ten games—and then we had the bowls. They used to vote for the national championship before the bowl. Then they started the program of voting *after* the bowls were played. There seemed to be less complaining about that system than any other system. But I never heard so many complaints as about the BCS in 2003. Somebody gets left out, and they make plenty of noise when they get left out.

Public Service

JW: *There's an area that we have not discussed. It was a major part of your activities while you were coach, and it still is today, I believe: all the charity work that you've been involved with over the years. When did you start getting involved in programs concerned with alcohol- and drug-abuse prevention?*

DR: Well, my wife, Edith, is more involved in that than I am. But I have taken several people to treatment centers, my friends, and talked to them about their problem and was able to convince them to go into treatment. And it worked. But the charity work, I tried to be involved in a little bit of it while I was working, but I didn't have enough time. My calendar's still pretty well filled with attending charity events and then conducting some of our own here in Austin at Barton Creek [Country Club] and being involved with some of the city projects.

I don't mean to sound like I'm doing more than my share of work, and I don't want to take credit for doing things that I don't do, but I am concerned about the community, I'm concerned about the state, and I'm concerned about people. Goodness! The good things that have happened to me—I think if I'm in a position to maybe put something back in the pot, I would be less than fair if I wouldn't be willing to do that, because I've certainly taken my share.

JW: *What sort of formal organization do you have to do your charitable work? Is there one?*

DR: No, I just pick and choose and just do it personally. I was instrumental in getting the Ben, Willie, and Darrell Golf Classic tournament here. We've raised money to put into east Austin.

JW: *What sort of things do these funds go into in east Austin? Any particular projects you know of?*

Royal, with his wife Edith, accepts the award for Austinite of the Year from the Greater Austin Chamber of Commerce, 1995. Darrell K Royal Papers, CAH, DI01495.

The Darrell Royal Vocational Training Workshop, Austin, Texas (late 1960s), benefiting those with cerebral palsy. Darrell K Royal Papers, CAH, DI01563.

DR: Oh, there's a whole bunch of 'em. The money goes to the Austin Community Foundation. It's a nonprofit, and we have a committee that works with the Austin Community Foundation, and they seek and receive applications for this money. And they give written reports on the cause that they're asking money for, and then the committee reviews 'em and selects the ones and distributes the money, and it all goes to east Austin. None of it is drained off for administrative cost. The committee volunteers to serve on that. The Austin Community Foundation charges nothing for their work. So the entire amount actually gets distributed over to the east side.

JW: *You say that your wife, Edith, was particularly active in starting a lot of this work, particularly in alcohol and drug rehabilitation.*

DR: I don't know that she started anything, but she's been active in programs that existed. [Edith was on the first board of the Palmer Drug Abuse Program, later called the Austin Drug Abuse Program. She is presently on the board of Austin Recovery.]

JW: *There was, back during your coaching days and until, I think, the 1970s, a Darrell Royal Center down on Congress Avenue [in Austin]. What was that?*

DR: Cerebral palsy. There was a Darrell Royal workshop, and I would go there on occasions, and we would do different things to raise money for the center. But mainly I was working then, and it was more of a name lending than it was actually getting in and doing a lot of the work.

JW: *So you say a great deal of your time around the calendar is spent in attending events that are for fund-raising?*

DR: I ask people to come and attend the different charities here. They have charities in their communities, and they ask me to come, so I have to respond, or I should respond. And I enjoy responding because they're doing a good job with their charity, also.

JW: *Yeah.*

DR: You know, you get involved in this, and then you become involved in other people's charities. They come to yours, and when they ask you, you go to theirs.

Freeport-McMoRan, Jim Bob Moffett, and Barton Springs

JW: *You mentioned the east Austin project, where you're raising funds for community development. These funds came from the Freeport-McMoRan Corporation. The president of that is Jim Bob Moffett, and he's one of your former players, is he not?*

DR: Yeah, that's correct, and that's the way I became involved in Barton Creek [Properties]. And then, being out here, I serve as the chairman of the board of governors because of Jim Bob. He got me involved. He's the CEO of Freeport-McMoRan, and they've been very generous with their money. They've moved into the Austin community, and they're trying to be a good community citizen. For instance, in New Orleans—they've been located in New Orleans now for many years— they've given more than $30 million to charities. And since they've moved into Austin in a business way, they've become sponsors of a lot of different events. They contribute money to a lot of different causes here in the city.

JW: *When did he play for you?*

DR: He was here in 1957. He was a freshman. He had already been recruited and a member of the squad. Then he played '58, '59, '60, and '61. He stayed for the full five years.

JW: *Obviously, the community of Austin has a lot of different voices being heard, and there was a real strong environmental movement, so a lot of controversies have been raised in some sectors of the Austin press about Freeport-McMoRan and other developers in Barton Creek. And so you and former chancellor William H. Cunningham, who are both associated with this, have received some flak from certain quarters. But did you feel those charges were unjustified?*

DR: I do, but I haven't been aware of receiving any flak. I guess there're

Jim Bob Moffett, who played for Royal from 1958–1961.
Texas Student Publications Photographs, CAH, DI01564.

some people out there talking about me. But give me credit for this: at least I'm doing what I think is right. I would not be a name-lender and I would not be a participant in anything that would harm this city and harm my reputation. I'm getting on up in years, and it took me a lot of years to establish what I *think* is an honest reputation for abiding by rules and being concerned about the city of Austin, and I'm not going to do anything to harm that reputation. Money won't cause me to do it. I'm a supporter of what's going on out here simply because I believe that we're doing it the right way. I think Freeport-McMoRan has the money to do it in a more environmentally sensitive way than other people would be willing to do or have the finances to do. I strongly believe that my endorsement is correct, and I'm totally confident with it. I think I'm doing something *for* the community as opposed to against the community.

JW: *I just wanted to give you a chance to sound off if you wanted to. [laughs]*

DR: I'm free to do that any time. I was given the assurance that they would not do anything to harm Barton Creek, which harms Barton Springs. This might interest you. University professors did a water quality study back in the 1920s. The water quality standards are the same now as they were back in 1920s with no development out here whatsoever. Most of the pollution that goes into Barton Creek is from wildlife, from the fecal coliform, birds, coyotes, coons, and deer. And when it rains, all that washes into the watershed, which is 350 square miles. It washes down, and then it has a way of purifying in that aquifer.

And Barton Creek [Properties] gets blamed for a lot of pollution when there's no development out there. There has been practically no development out there. The old development that was developed under no regulations, that's where the problem is, if there's a problem, but still, the water quality hasn't been degraded.

JW: *One of the areas that environmentalists often focus on when they criticize developments is golf courses, which I know are very close to your heart—and runoff and fertilizers and whatnot. I would just ask this one question: do they have one single water test to prove it?*

DR: They just make the accusation and don't have to prove it. Freeport-McMoRan spent over a million dollars in water tests. They know what's going on. The golf course actually serves as a filter. We've tested the water that runs off from bare land, tested it just before it hits the rough. Then after it goes through the rough of the fairway and then goes through the fairway and goes through the rough on the other side and then into the creek—tested it before it goes into the creek. And the water is better there than it is coming off of raw land. So, no, the golf courses are not doing anything to hurt that creek.

You know, it's a funny thing, too, some of these environmentalists. They talk about spraying with effluent [treated sewage]. And they just raise Cain about its being sprayed with effluent. The effluent tests better than the water out of the Colorado River, because it's treated, and the same people who are complaining about effluent being used out here to irrigate the golf courses are advocating that it be used on the Jimmy Clay golf course.

JW: *Which is a downtown Austin golf course.*

DR: Yeah, and they're pushing them to use effluent to water the golf course. That's the recommended way to *use* effluent, is in irrigation.

JW: *Yeah.*

DR: It's treated water.

JW: *So you've sort of kept up on this, have you? [laughs]*

DR: Yeah. Well, I don't know if you want this on tape, but we had the Texas Water Commission—I've forgotten the name of it now—it's a different name now, but they came out to test the water. [In 1993 the Texas Water Commission and the Texas Air Control Board were merged into the Texas Natural Resource Conservation Commission, which in 2002 became the Texas Commission on Environmental Quality.] They came at a surprise time, and they tested the water at the sprinkler head, the water that was going out. And so they go and conduct their tests, and then they come back and say, "Well, you're putting water out that's not the quality that you told us it was. Here are the tests, and this is what we've found." They said, "Well, what date did you make this test?" They gave the date.

We go back and check our records. We alternately use effluent and then use water out of the river. That was the day that we were watering out of the river, so they were testing water, water out of the Colorado River. We said, "OK, now come back and test us when we're on the effluent." They came back, tested us, and said, "You're right where you said you were." So the effluent is better than the quality of the water coming out of the river, out of Lake Austin.

JW: *Let's get the name right. Is it Barton Creek Country Club?*

DR: Well, Barton Creek Properties. It's a club, it's a spa, it's a hotel, it's golf courses, and it's development. See, they own about 9,000 acres. They donated the Sweetwater [Ranch] and Uplands tracts to the city. [Note: These tracts were actually donated to the Nature Conservancy of Texas.] But, then, they own a lot of land to be developed, plus these other facilities that I've mentioned. So the total is called Barton Creek Properties.

JW: *OK.*

DR: It's not just the golf course. Now just the golf course itself is Barton Creek Country Club. It's like Austin Country Club. You know, that's the strange thing. Austin Country Club is right on the water. Not a word is ever said about their golf course, because they don't have a bad guy. They've got their bad guy in Jim Bob Moffett and a big rich company [like] Freeport-McMoRan.

JW: *Yeah.*

DR: It would have been pretty hard for them to jump on Harvey Penick. [Penick, a legendary UT golf coach and teacher, was long associated with the Austin Country Club.]

JW: *[laughs] Yeah, it would.*

DR: So they just don't say anything about the Austin Country Club. Just Barton Creek Country Club; that's doing all the damage.

JW: *Have you had any occasion to talk with Jim Bob Moffett about his feelings about the controversies here?*

DR: Oh, heck yeah, I talk to him all the time. See, he came in here and bought this land. He was the first one to show any confidence in the economy of Austin. This is when things were bad. He came in and bought it from savings institutions that had reclaimed it. All the politicians came out and had big ceremonies thanking him for coming to town, showing confidence in Austin. He expected to come in here and have an environmentally sensitive development and wear a white hat.

Well, after he got it bought and after they said, "Thank you for buying it and taking it off our hands," then the whole work from that time on was to try to keep him from doing anything with the land. Pay taxes on it, keep it up, but keep it bare. Don't put anything on it. It doesn't make sense. It's all over emotions. It's emotions and perception. It's not based on facts.

And they come and they just make these statements: "Golf courses pollute." According to who? They won't tell you what they put on the city golf courses. It's managed by the city. They won't tell you what kind of fertilizers and what kind of treatment they use there. You can't get that information. Nobody's tested the runoff of *their* water. It all goes into the same place. Only thing is, they jumped on the emotional thing of Barton Springs.

JW: *Yeah.*

DR: The crown jewel.

JW: *Right.*

DR: That came as a total surprise to everyone. When the development application was first submitted to the city, the controversy was all over songbirds. It was the black-capped vireo and the golden-cheeked warbler. Lo and behold, two days before the public hearing they say Barton Springs is in danger. That was the first time Barton Springs had ever been mentioned by anybody. It was a clever move that they used. And after you start answering the questions about Barton Springs, they come with the salamander. So they're gonna find something all the time. This fight's going on all over the nation. This is not confined to the city of Austin.

JW: *Was Moffett embittered or disillusioned at his experience?*

DR: No. No, he was a little bit hurt, but he's a big boy. He's been in business before, and he's had those run-ins before. He had the same thing in New Orleans. But he just kept doing what he feels is the right things for the right reasons, and now he's a hero in New Orleans. He's a big, big man in the city of New Orleans. They didn't accept him freely to begin with.

JW: *Helped the ailing economies?*

DR: That's right.

Catching the Cheaters

JW: *I saw an interesting interview with the* Daily Texan *back when you were still athletic director. Apparently, there were a lot of problems nationwide with recruiting violations and other rules violations, and you had been suggesting regularly the use of lie detectors in athletic departments to keep people on the straight and narrow. Do you recall advocating that?*

DR: Yeah, I'll tell you.

JW: *Did you say that flippantly or were you serious about it?*

DR: No, I wasn't flippant about it at all. For some reason, and probably for good reasons, it's not admissible in court, but I still see where they give the polygraph because it really is to catch a guy lying. So it's more appropriately named when you call it a lie detector, because if you're going to catch people who are cheating, you have to basically catch a liar. He's not going to tell you the truth if he's cheating. An absconder won't just say, "Oh, yeah, you caught me, I stole this money." Or "Yeah, oh yeah, I murdered the guy. Well, you caught me, I murdered him, yeah." They all say they didn't do it. They all say that they've been falsely accused. But before I took that stand, I took a polygraph test. I had a good polygraph operator come in, and he gave it to everybody on our coaching staff.

JW: *Really?*

DR: Yes, including myself. I was the first one to take it. And I failed the first test. He asked me—and you could just answer yes or no—if I had ever given money to students at the University of Texas. And I said no. Well, it struck me immediately that I had my son and daughter in college. I'd helped a nephew. And sure enough, it showed.

JW: *Even that?*

DR: Yeah. Because if he had said "athletes," I could've answered it.

JW: *Yeah.*

DR: So I went ahead with the test, and I said, just as soon as the thing was over, I said, "Say, you asked me a question, and you told me just to answer yes or no and go on through the test." I said, "That might show something there if this thing works, that I wasn't truthful when you asked if I'd ever helped any students at the University of Texas. Hell, I got my kids in school, I've helped a nephew through school, I've helped some ordinary students with finances."

JW: *Yeah.*

DR: I said, "You need to put 'student athlete' or 'athletes.'" So, then we gave it to everybody on the coaching staff.

JW: *How did they feel about that?*

DR: They didn't much like it.

JW: *[laughs] I can imagine.*

DR: And we found some little minor discrepancies. And several of the guys just took it and just went right on through it. But two guys, on little minor discrepancies, had something that they were hiding. It really didn't amount to a hill of beans. They just broke down and just had to confess to it and, then they went back on the test and cleared it. So I was convinced, but I was also convinced that a polygraph is no better than an operator. You get an incompetent operator, then you've got a test that's no good.

JW: *Yeah, the questions you ask, the way you ask them.*

DR: The questions you ask. And polygraph operators can be had, too. You know, you can't say that everyone is honest that runs a polygraph test. But I told the guy I wanted him to find everything he could. And so I believed in 'em, and then I got to thinking, well, you're not trying to find a cheater. You're trying to find a liar, because if a guy cheats, he's obligated to lie. So the best way to get him is a polygraph test. They're not admissible in court. They used 'em some in the Southwest Conference, but they never did initiate it in the right way.

JW: *Were they responding to a particular crisis in athletic departments? Why were they even worried about trying to ferret out liars? What brought out all this interest?*

DR: *I* brought it out. I was the one who got all that going; I really and truly wanted to clean up intercollegiate athletics and get the people who were buying athletes out. It was either that or quit myself, because you can't compete with 'em.

JW: *What kind of reaction did you get from athletic departments around the conference?*

DR: Oh, some of 'em didn't want to take it.

JW: *[laughs] I can imagine.*

DR: You know, and then some of 'em said, "Well, I took it and I passed it."

JW: *[laughs] So this also went outside the conference?*

DR: Yeah. But that was all a mess. I don't know whether I'd advocate that again or not. It's kind of controversial. They claim that they're about 90 percent accurate. But 90 percent accuracy is still a hell of a lot better than anything any investigator's been able to do.

JW: *Yeah.*

DR: See, what I advocated was, give the polygraph test. Let each department give their own and let them keep that private the first year. Let them find out what's going on *in* their department. Then the next year, the conference can go give it to each school; get rid of these investigators who are traveling around. Just take the polygraph test in and give it to 'em. I said, "They're going to find out that there's enough things wrong in their department. Give it in secret so that they can keep the information and they're not obligated to give it to anybody." Now the next year they know that the conference is going to come in and give 'em a polygraph test. You won't find any of those coaches going out there breaking any rules. It'll eliminate it, and I still believe it would.

Mike Campbell

The UT coaching staff from the early 1960s. Top row, from left: Bill Ellington, Charley Shira, Bob Schulze, Jim Pittman, Russell Coffee. Bottom row, from left: T. Jones, Darrell Royal, Mike Campbell. Photography by Laughead Photographers. Texas Student Publications Photographs, CAH, CN02134.

JW: *The late Mike Campbell was one of your assistant coaches for many years. When did he join your coaching staff?*

DR: In 1956, when I went to the University of Washington.

JW: *Oh, you brought him with you from Washington.*

DR: Yeah, I hired him. He was coaching high school football in Mississippi when I was coaching at Mississippi State. And I got to know him, was very much impressed with him, and I asked him to go to the University of Washington with me, which he did. We were there less than a year. Then I got a chance to come to Texas, and he came with me and was with me here for the full twenty years. That was the best thing to ever happen to me: Mike was as good a football man as I've ever been around.

JW: *I believe you were hoping that he might take over your coaching duties when you retired as head coach.*

DR: Well, I thought he had a chance, but that wasn't my selection. That was up to the board of regents. They decided they'd do the picking. That's the way I was hired, too, so, I guess fair's fair.

JW: *When you stepped down from coaching and then later from athletic director, what did he do at that time?*

DR: He went to work for the Texas Teachers Retirement System. And then when they formed the Texas Longhorn Educational Foundation, he resigned that job there and went to work for them.

JW: *How was that TLEF set up? Whose initiative was that, to create that?*

DR: It was a number of boosters. Just a good way to contribute money.

JW: *Did you have any role in that?*

DR: Not really. I had some input that Mike be hired, but not really, no.

After Royal

JW: *When John Mackovic came in as head football coach, did you have any input into his hiring?*

DR: I was on the interviewing panel. Well, I was invited to go to Chicago, where we interviewed him.

JW: *What other candidates do you recall having considered?*

DR: He was the only one we talked to.

JW: *Is that right?*

DR: Um-hmm. He was the only one who was interviewed.

JW: *That is interesting.*

DR: Now, DeLoss Dodds talked to some other people, but that particular group interviewed only one coach. But DeLoss had done a lot of work on talking to other people.

JW: *Screening the applicants?*

DR: Yeah, and some of them, I think, dropped out from interviews.

JW: *The football team has had a series of head coaches since your departure from coaching. Were you very much involved with the football program during those years?*

After the UT-Oklahoma game in 1999, the Longhorns and coach Mack Brown presented Royal with the game ball. UT overcame a seventeen-point deficit in one of the biggest comebacks in school history to defeat the Sooners 38–28. It was Coach Brown's 100th career victory. Darrell K Royal Papers, CAH, DI01518.

DR: No, I haven't been very much involved any time. Mack Brown and his staff have been so cordial and so nice to me. When I go to a practice or drop by the office, they're just nice as they can be. But still, I don't have anything to do with any kind of input. They don't need it. It's been a long time, and my mind may be a little rusty as far as the technical side of football. The terminology and all has changed so much. Gosh, you know, it's been twenty-seven years now [in 2004] since I coached. I haven't had any involvement at all since I left the sideline.

JW: *The head coaches have been Fred Akers, then David McWilliams, John Mackovic, and finally now Mack Brown. Mack Brown seems to be the coach that's reached out and pulled you back in the program.*

DR: Well, the other people were nice to me, too. But I've said this about Mack: I think he fits the University of Texas as well as any person could. DeLoss Dodds deserves the credit for selecting Mack. As a matter of fact, DeLoss has got a tremendous coaching staff all the way around. Every sport is doing well. We're winning conference championships. We're not on probation; we're not breaking rules; our coaches are doing a great job; and we're just lucky to have all the coaches we have now at the University of Texas.

JW: *In fact, as we speak, in the summer of 2004, the UT Longhorn baseball team is at the College World Series, about to play its semifinal.*

DR: You bet. I'm anxious to be in front of the television when they play this afternoon. [The Longhorns beat Georgia in the semifinals, but lost to Cal State–Fullerton, two games to none, in the championship series.]

Fred Steinmark

JW: *Coach, there's a really dramatic story that we have not put down for the record here, and that's one of your players from back in the late 1960s, Fred Steinmark. Of course, the scoreboard is named in his memory today. For the record, he was a player who was stricken with cancer and eventually died, but he was in that famous Texas-Arkansas game in 1969, was he not?*

DR: He was. I remember when he was recruited. He weighed only about 150 pounds, but I never talked to him [about it], never. I knew what he weighed. There wasn't any need in me asking him or bringing it up. We either wanted him or we didn't want him. So there's no need saying, "Well, you're pretty small, but we're going to take you anyway." So I recruited him just like we did everybody else: enthusiastically. He said that that was one thing he always appreciated, that I never mentioned his size. He weighed as much as I did when I started as a freshman at the University of Oklahoma, so I never did put much stock in the size.

JW: *What position did he play?*

DR: He was defensive safety for us and the punt returner. And the coaching staff had noticed that he'd kind of lost a step of speed there in his senior year. From about midseason on, he couldn't quite cover the same ground. He played against Arkansas, in that game of 1969. Matter of fact, he was defeated on a pass, and he did one of the more intelligent things that a player could do. I mean, he deliberately tackled the guy, interfered with him. It's better to get a penalty than a touchdown, and it would've been a certain touchdown. He interfered with him, and we held.

But we'd substituted Rick Nabors, who eventually replaced him for the Cotton Bowl. Rick played quite a bit in that game because we'd noticed, again, that Freddie had lost a step of speed. Immediately after that ball game, he went

*Longhorn player Fred Steinmark on the field at the Cotton Bowl in 1970.
Prints and Photographs Collection, CAH, CN09792.*

*Steinmark and Royal after the
Longhorns' Cotton Bowl victory over Notre Dame.
Darrell K Royal Papers, CAH, DI01488.*

straight to Frank Medina, our trainer, and said, "Frank, my leg's been hurting. And the pain is getting bad, and I want to know what's wrong." Frank sent him to a doctor in Austin. They took an X-ray, and immediately they took him to M. D. Anderson Hospital in Houston.

This was after the Arkansas game. I was in New York with the co-captains. We were up there receiving the MacArthur Trophy, which was symbolic of a national championship. And Dr. Charles A. LeMaistre, who was our chancellor at that time, came to me and said, "I've got some bad news. I need to talk to you in private." And he took me from that celebration of receiving that trophy, took me around into the other room and said, "Freddie Steinmark has gone to M. D. Anderson. They've taken X-rays, and they're just certain that it's cancer. They're not going to say so until they go in and take a biopsy. But if they find it to be benign, this will be the first case that we've seen with X-rays like this that's benign." He said, "The prognosis is that he'll have to have his leg amputated, and that he'll probably have two years after that."

And so Freddie plays in a football game on Saturday, and on Monday he's taking X-rays. In less than a week, he's lost his leg.

JW: *That's a vicious turn of events.*

DR: It's a vicious turn of events, but the doctor said that that bone was so eaten and it was so thin—was hanging by just a shred. Said, "It could've broken stepping off of a curb." They didn't understand how it could not have been broken in the process of that game.

JW: *Playing the game, yeah.*

DR: And they said had his muscle structure not been so good and held and supported his leg, there's no way he could've run or done anything. It was almost eaten through, and it was just gonna give way in time, anyway. So that kid played with that leg, played in a ball game, and in less than a week they've amputated it. Freddie was a tough little fighter.

JW: *You went to visit him afterwards.*

DR: Oh sure, sure.

JW: *And he also made an appearance.*

DR: At the team banquet. When his leg was amputated, he said, "What kind of program can I get on? I want to go to the Cotton Bowl. I want to go and be on the sideline." The doctors, they thought, "No way. We've never had

Steinmark walks across the stage at the Longhorn awards show in the spring of 1970. Left to right: Jack Blanton, Darrell Royal, Rooster Andrews, Steinmark, and Scott Henderson. Darrell K Royal Papers, CAH, DI01505.

a patient recover that fast." He said, "I'm gonna go. I want to." So they had a prosthesis, and he exercised and did everything to get up enough strength to go to that game, and he was on the sideline at the game—on crutches, of course.

JW: *I remember that, yes.*

DR: The doctors changed their way of getting people back on their feet, based on what Freddie did, because they knew it could be done. They didn't think it could be done. They told him; they were honest. They said, "We were honest with him." They said, "Freddie, we don't think you can." He said, "I'll do it."

JW: *Well, he also showed up at the team banquet.*

DR: When he showed up at the banquet to receive his letter award, he had a cane. But he walked across there with his prosthesis. They'd *never* had anybody walk that soon.

JW: *Yeah. The fact that he was an athlete, I'm sure, contributed to that.*

DR: Scott Henderson, one of his teammates, walked alongside him. He didn't hold him. He was there just in case. Scott was a real, real close friend of his. Little Freddie used a cane, and he walked right across that floor. He wanted to get his letter award, and he wanted to walk. And he did.

JW: *How long did he survive after that?*

DR: He died almost two years [later], to the day.

JW: *So they were very accurate in their picture.*

DR: They were extremely accurate.

JW: *Yeah.*

DR: Sad part of it is that that kind of cancer can be cured now. Research has found a cure for that particular cancer. They don't amputate anymore.

JW: *His was in the very advanced stage, though.*

DR: Oh, he played on that thing all season long. There's no telling how much pain that kid had. The cancer had eaten through his leg. They said there was just a sliver of bone on both sides. Freddie Steinmark is a great name to go down in the history of athletics at the University of Texas. I'm glad that scoreboard is there, named after him, and with a beautiful inscription.

[The inscription on the Fred Steinmark scoreboard at Royal-Memorial Stadium reads as follows:

DEDICATED TO THE MEMORY OF FRED STEINMARK
1949–1971

Defensive back of the Texas Longhorn national football champions of 1969, whose courageous fight against savage odds transcended the locker room, the playing field, the campus, the nation itself. The indelible memory of his indomitable spirit will ever provide an inspiration to those who play the game or live a life.]

Remembering Katy

JW: *Just for the record here, what's the story behind your middle initial, "K"?*

DR: The K was for my mother, whose name was Katy. Her name was Katy Elizabeth. And they just put in the initial only, but that's what it was for. My mother died when I was four months old, so I never knew her. But it's kind of interesting that later in high school I wound up with the nickname "Katy," and any time I hear somebody say, "Hey, Katy!" I know that it's somebody from high school days. But they didn't even know that my mother's name was Katy and that that was what it was for. There was a railroad line that came through, the MKT Railroad—Missouri, Kansas, and Texas—and it came through Hollis. And they called it "the Katy." But because of the K in the middle of MKT and DKR, from that sprung the name Katy.

JW: *Is that right? [laughs]*

DR: It had to do with a railroad, and they didn't know that my mother's name was Katy. I think that started in junior high—somebody talking about the Katy railroad line.

JW: *Well, they like you in Hollis today, don't they?*

DR: [laughs] I don't know. I would like to think they do. I've always enjoyed going home. Of course, the friends that I know and knew and grew up with, many of 'em have died. Gosh, it's more than fifty years now since I lived in that little town of 2,500 people. I've always gone back. I still go back today. And I still have a lot of friends around there. But nothing like I used to. You know, in fifty years so many things change. But oh yeah, I can go down and sit at the Hollis Inn early in the morning, and I can see about everybody I know. There's some of 'em still around. But most of the old-timers who I knew, who I used to shine their shoes, they're gone.

But it was a great little place to grow up. I had wonderful high school teachers and my high school coach, Dick Highfill, was great. I called him a few years ago, when he was eighty-five years old. He was living in Alva, Oklahoma. He didn't believe me at first. When I called him, I said, "Coach, this is Darrell Royal." He said, "Yeah?" And I could tell that he thought somebody was pulling his leg. So I just kept on talking. And I started talking about things, you know, from the past, and he quickly caught on. He was convinced quickly. I'm sure he knew my voice because I certainly remembered him. I hadn't seen him in twenty years, but I recognized *his* voice. I could spot it just like that.

JW: *In 1996 the university's board of regents added your name to Memorial Stadium. How did you feel about that?*

DR: Well, you can imagine how a coach would feel. A place where he had worked for twenty years and had been in that stadium many, many times in practices and games. For any coach to have a stadium named after him is a big thrill. I was just totally amazed when they came to me and told me that they had proposed, and the regents had agreed, to put my name on the stadium. I was just dumbfounded, and I just sat there, and finally Bill Cunningham, the chancellor, said, "Well, we have to have your approval." [laughs] So I said, "You're waiting on my approval to put my name on the stadium? The answer is yes. I didn't know I was supposed to respond."

JW: *How did you hear about it?*

DR: Chancellor Cunningham and the president, Robert Berdahl, came to my house and told me. I didn't know anything about it. I had no idea that was in the making or being considered. To have my name added to the stadium is quite a thrill.

JW: *And now I understand that something along those same lines has occurred back in your old hometown, Hollis, Oklahoma.*

DR: Yeah, they named the high school field after me in my hometown this past season [November 2003], and I was very honored to have that happen. There was a doctor in Hollis—matter of fact, the doctor who delivered me—

The former coach and athletic director was honored in 1996 when the football field was renamed the Darrell K Royal–Texas Memorial Stadium. Photograph by Susan Sigmon, UT Sports Information Department. Darrell K Royal Papers, CAH, DI01565.

Dr. Will Husband. It's Will Husband Stadium and Darrell K Royal Field. Like Darrell Royal Stadium and Joe Jamail Field. The same deal.

JW: *Going back to the Memorial Stadium honor, was there some sort of public program?*

DR: We had a day where we went out on the field and they named the stadium. But having the name up there was way more important than that ceremony. [laughs]

JW: *Well, Coach, you've been a recipient of lots of honors. The Memorial Stadium, of course, was one thing. I know that you're a member of the Horatio Alger Association, and they have an annual award, which I understand that you received in 1996. How did that come about?*

DR: Well, I don't know. They just notified me that I'd been selected, and it is really quite an event. They help underprivileged children with their college expenses. They select kids who have been in trouble, kids who need a helping hand. They invite them to come to the Horatio Alger dinner, and money from that goes to scholarships for those young people.

JW: *I also understand that you and your wife, Edith, won the Harvey Penick Award in 1999. What does that involve?*

DR: Well, that was a great honor to receive. It's really a nice trophy, and Harvey Penick was such a wonderful person. It's a Caritas of Austin charity award. Harvey was a golf pro at the Austin Country Club and coach of the University of Texas golf team for many years.

JW: *Several years ago,* Texas Monthly *published an article about the notion of "the good ol' boy."* Texas Monthly *gave the term "good ol' boy" a positive definition. They had categories of who were* really *good ol' boys and who were the wannabes. You were cited as a model of the true good ol' boy in this article. To* Texas Monthly, *that means you're honorable, you're a straight shooter, you're not full of yourself, and you aren't full of a false pride and things like that. There's a humility, an ability to be one of the people, looking out for the underdogs, all sorts of positive qualities. Did you feel like that was an accurate reflection of who you are?*

DR: Well, I've always known that I'm greatly influenced by my father, greatly influenced by my high school superintendent, principals, and teachers, and my football coaches in my younger days. I always studied those people who I admired and tried anyway to do as they taught. I've always liked people.

I enjoy talking to people. I know sometimes people will stop me and say, "I don't want to bother you now, I don't want to bother," but they're not bothering me. I'm flattered. But I don't know. It's a hard thing when someone has given you a tag and then for you to try to explain it. So I'm not very good at that.

JW: *I think we've covered our agenda. I sure appreciate it, Coach. Thank you very much.*

DR: Thank you kindly.